US TAX REFORM AND INVESTMENT

To my parents.

US Tax Reform
and Investment

Reality and rhetoric in the 1980s

JULIE ANN ELSTON
Wissenschaftszentrum Berlin für Sozialforschung

Avebury

Aldershot • Brookfield USA • Hong Kong • Singapore • Sydney

Published by
Avebury
Ashgate Publishing Limited
Gower House
Croft Road
Aldershot
Hants GU11 3HR
England

Ashgate Publishing Company
Old Post Road
Brookfield
Vermont 05036
USA

A CIP catalogue record for this book is available from the British Library

Library of Congress Catalog Card Number: 94-80264

ISBN 1 85628 948 6

Printed and bound by Athenæum Press Ltd., Gateshead, Tyne & Wear.

Contents

List of tables

List of figures

Acknowledgments

The author wishes to sincerely thank Horst Albach, Rabah Amir and David Audretsch, for insightful comments on earlier versions of this manuscript. I would also like to thank Erik Beck, Nina Bonge, Marie-Antoinette Eggebrecht, and Alois Weidinger for technical advice and assistance in preparing this text. This research effort was driven by conversations I had with Homer Spence, who convinced me that economists should have a more active role in analyzing and commenting on American policy. Financial support is gratefully acknowledged from the University of Washington, the Center for Social Science Computation and Research (CSSCR), and the Wissenschaftszentrum Berlin (WZB). The opinions and interpretations presented are my own and do not necessarily reflect those of any institutions with which I am associated. Any omissions or errors remain my responsiblilty.

1 Introduction

In 1980, when Ronald Reagan announced his plan to alleviate America's economic woes through painless tax cuts to promote real economic growth, most Americans were willing to believe him. This faith stemmed not only from Reagan's forceful and appealing advocacy on this issue, but from the understanding that these feats were easily attainable under his new supply-side economic plan.[1] Reagan's supply-side argument can be summarized as follows. Lower marginal tax rates will result in higher tax revenues if the lower rate provides such a stimulation to savings and investment that total taxes collected are greater in spite of the lower new tax rate. This means that cuts in the personal income tax rates would stimulate individuals' work efforts, and business tax cuts would encourage investment.[2] Both of these effects were to have increased capital formation, resulting in productivity growth while restoring US competitiveness abroad. And all of this was to occur while reducing the federal deficit at home, because tax receipts from a growing economy would be even greater than before. While theoretically possible, this sequence of events failed to materialize.

Instead the record federal deficits during the 1980s were accompanied by sluggish productivity growth and a disappointing lack of capital formation. In fact, net business capital formation was significantly lower during every year of the 1980s than it has been for the last three decades on average.[3]

Further, these disappointing results had come at the cost of likely tax increases in the future, since reducing taxes at the time also reduced federal tax revenues needed to finance the burgeoning deficit. What happened? Somewhere between political promises and economic possibilities, the alchemy of turning tax cuts into investment growth did not transform into reality. Exactly what happened to business capital formation in the 1980s? Why didn't our costly tax cuts result in the expected increase in investment that would turn our economy around rather than slowing it to a state of stagnation?

One answer is that what is economically possible is not necessarily the inevitable or even the most likely outcome. The administration's plan was theoret-

1

ically possible, yet unlikely to succeed for many reasons which will be explored in this study, including assumptions made about the growth rate of economic factors in response to economic incentives.[4]

Many policy makers as well as citizens were dismayed that the tax-based policy incentives were followed by an increase in the budget deficit, low investment rates and faltering productivity growth. And if policy makers and administration experts had trouble evaluating the probable sequence of events, how could the average American citizen possibly be expected to determine the reasonableness of the claims made about the magnitude of economic growth to be expected?

The purpose of this book is to clarify the historical development of the interaction between tax reforms and investment in the 1980s, as well as to provide a framework for evaluating future tax-based policy programs aimed at increasing US investment and productivity. By examining both aggregate and individual firm investment behaviour, it is hoped this work will shed some light on the complex relationship between tax-based policy incentives and the firm's decision to invest within the context of the economic environment prevailing in the 1980s. By improving our understanding of the relationship between tax cuts and investment growth we should be better able to evaluate the fiscal policy claims of politicians and demand responsibility in terms of their campaign promises and our tax dollars.

Chapter 2 discusses the underpinning of the theory of tax-stimulated investment growth, showing how, in these particular circumstances, the tax policies were ineffective at the aggregate level in alleviating the economic problems of the 1980s.

Chapter 3 examines each of the tax reform acts of the 1980s in order to investigate the impacts each of the acts had on investment decisions. This chapter analyzes the effectiveness of the tax reforms with respect to their impact on the growth of the capital stock of the firm, the equity of the tax burden, and the neutrality of taxation with respect to the different types of capital investment as well as inflation. Evaluating the overall success or failure of these tax reforms in terms of capital formation realized is an important task in spite of the statistical problems and limitations encountered in doing so for several reasons. From an economist's perspective, the frequent reforms of the 1980s render it an ideal period to study the effects of fiscal policy tax shocks on investment behaviour over time. For policy makers it is important to determine the effectiveness of tax reforms in addressing the problems of capital formation and stimulation. For tax-payers perhaps the most important question is, did we get what we paid for?

Chapter 4 outlines the Q theory of investment framework which is used to empirically examine firm investment behaviour. A model of the firm is also developed, incorporating the impact of the marginal personal income tax rate as well as the dividend payment of the firm.

2

Chapter 5 develops the link between the theoretical model of the firm and a specification in terms of observable parameters so that empirical testing is possible.

Chapter 6 investigates the validity of the Q theory of investment model, using a panel data set of US firms over time. This chapter also develops an econometric methodology for analyzing investment behaviour at the firm level over time.

Chapter 7 discusses considerations for future tax reforms in the US, investigating the feasibility and impact of alternative tax reforms for stimulating firm investment and productivity, while maintaining revenue neutrality at the federal level.

Overall, empirical results confirm the widespread suspicion that the link between the tax reforms and investment growth in the 1980s was weak. This observation is supported by lack of correspondence between movements in the aggregate growth rate of investment and movements in the firm's marginal incentive to invest as measured by the tax-adjusted Q.

Results also support the hypothesis that recent revisions in the tax code have included a sort of mixed bag of tax-based incentive effects, which tended to cancel each other out, providing an unclear signal to firms on investment. The implication is that future tax reform will have to consider more carefully the precise mix of incentives. A cohesive package on investment incentives for the firm should evaluate the *net* impact to the firm of all the reforms, rather than focus on individual provisions, ignoring conflicting effects of other reform measures.

Analysis of firm behaviour using panel data indicates that liquidity constraints, as measured by firm cash flow, are indeed an important determinant of investment. This result was strengthened by the fact that cash flow was significant even when controlling for dividend payout behaviour of the firm. One implication of this finding is that it would be advantageous for future policy makers to consider the impacts of tax reform on the firm's liquidity constraint when considering investment incentives. Policy makers could effectively argue that measures to loosen the firm's liquidity constraints may also increase capital formation. In spite of the formidable challenge of policy makers in the 1990s, we benefit by analyzing the difficulties of the previous efforts. These lessons of the 1980s about what did and did not work are important when considering directions for tax reform in the 1990s. What is also important is to consider new tax alternatives or policy measures to increase savings, investment and overall productivity without worsening the federal deficit. One source of alternative ideas is examples provided by other countries which are more successful in balancing their revenue needs with investment incentives.

3

Notes

1. Ironically, one of Reagan's strongest critics was George Bush, who later continued these same policies in his own presidency, thus magnifying the impact of Reagan's policies beyond what even he had envisioned.

2. Average tax burdens could be higher or lower under the Reagan plan.

3. See the *National Income and Product Accounts*, 1959-88.

4. Many economists have also pointed to the Federal Reserve Bank (Fed) as making problems worse by failing to support the administration's plans. While this criticism may be warranted, the Fed's job in guiding monetary policy is rarely directed by fiscal goals. In fact, by design, the Fed has a directive to focus on problems such as stabilizing interest rates and controlling inflation.

2 The theory of tax-based investment growth

'...the idea that cutting taxes will result in higher revenues, and increased investment, is just nonsense. It's Voodoo Economics...'

George Bush

America's transition from the 1970s to the 1980s

To understand what happened in America during the 1980s it is important to look at both beginning and ending conditions in addition to the process which took place in between.

The 1970s had not been a star decade for the US in terms of economic performance, and the 1980s were seen as the decade when clever policies would be wielded to turn things around. The 1981 *Economic Report of the President* eagerly detailed the new administration's bold new plan to address the nation's declining rate of productivity growth as well as increase the share of national resources allocated to capital formation. This came in the wake of sobering reports that America was lagging behind other industrialized countries in terms of its competitive position in the world market place. In truth, the US was lagging behind the UK, Italy, Germany, France and Japan in terms of its investment and productivity growth. The relative performance of the US compared to other industrialized countries during the 1970s is depicted in Figure 2.1.

This cross-country comparison also addresses concerns that US performance was due to factors primarily outside its control, such as the oil shocks of the 1970s. Since all the industrial countries presumably faced these and other exogenous factors together, this allows us to see how others performed in the world arena which set the stage for the 1980s.

5

Comparing productivity using the growth rate of output per hour in the manufacturing sector across countries, the US had the lowest productivity rate, at nearly half that of Germany or Italy, and about a third of Japan's. Similarly, if we examine net fixed investment as a percentage of the total Gross Domestic Product (GDP) for each country, the US again finished last, devoting a smaller fraction of its total output to new investment than any other industrialized nation in the study. It is apparent from this international comparison that the US was already lagging behind other countries in terms of investment and productivity before Reagan took office in 1981. Having recognized these problems, he set out to form a comprehensive economic plan which focused on providing investment incentives to stimulate capital formation, increase productivity and restore international competitiveness.

Supply-side economics

The Reagan administration believed that tax rates were too high, and that the government sector was too large. The resulting supply-side program which they instituted was based on the following claims:

1. Income taxes reduce the after-tax return to work effort.

2. An increase in the after-tax return to work and saving will create a *significant* increase in the amount of work and saving.

3. The resulting increase in work and saving will be so significant, that even after the proposed tax cuts, the federal government will collect more tax revenue than before the cuts.

The first statement is non-controversial, as everyone agrees that taxes reduce incentives to work. However, the second claim was, and continues to be disputed by many economists. In fact if one compares the situation 4 years before the tax cuts to the situation after the tax cuts, the amount of work effort, as measured by the labor-force participation rate, grew more slowly after 1981 than before, and the rate of personal savings fell after rising during 1977-1978. The third claim is related to the predictions of the infamous Laffer curve, named after economist Arthur Laffer. This curve describes the situation where no tax revenues are collected with either a zero tax rate or a 100 percent tax rate. The optimal rate, from a tax revenue perspective, lies somewhere between the two end points of the curve, but where exactly the optimal point lies is unclear.

The large structural deficit which emerged in the 1980s was the result of the administration's program of reducing tax rates while increasing (defense) spend-

6

ing. According to Gordon (1987), government spending as a percentage of the Gross National Product (GNP) remained higher in the 1982-1985 period, than in any postwar year prior to 1982. Further, this deficit had developed in a time of peace rather than war, and expansion rather than recession.

The role of debt and savings

When Reagan took office in 1981 the federal budget deficit was nearly $80 billion. However, due to federal spending that was consistently higher than revenues, by the end of the decade the deficit had grown to $2.6 trillion in spite of the fact that upon entering office he pledged that his number one goal was to 'control the runaway deficit'. This tremendous growth in the federal deficit during such a relatively short period had several deleterious effects on investment growth and productivity, as well as the overall health of the economy.

First, the high deficit led to higher real interest rates, which 'crowded out' private investment and hindered capital formation. This hurt productivity because in order for it to increase, workers needed both *more* and *newer* capital equipment which embodies a higher technology.

Second, as the deficit grew it also absorbed more and more of national savings. Because the rate of saving did not increase, this caused heavy borrowing from abroad. One side effect of this borrowing is that foreigners now own more of American resources than ever before in history. Figure 2.2 depicts the relationship between gross savings and investment as a percentage of the Gross National Product from 1947 to 1987.

From Figure 2.2 it is clear that, as a percentage of the GNP, savings and investment did not increase in the 1980s. They have continued to be on the decline since the late 1970s right on through the 1980s where gross savings remained below the historical trend. From Figure 2.2 it is also clear how strong the relationship is between savings and investment. Figure 2.2 also illustrates how federal dissavings have been chipping away at investment at an increasing rate. Federal dissavings, or the difference between federal spending and revenue as a percentage of the GNP, was -2.1 percent in 1981, -4.6 percent in 1982, -5.2 percent in 1983, -4.5 percent in 1984, and -5 percent in 1985.[1]

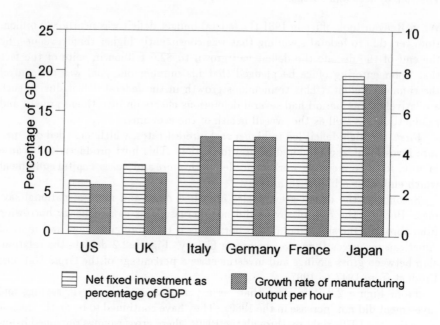

Figure 2.1: **International capital formation and productivity 1971-1980**
Source: Economic Report of the President (1983).

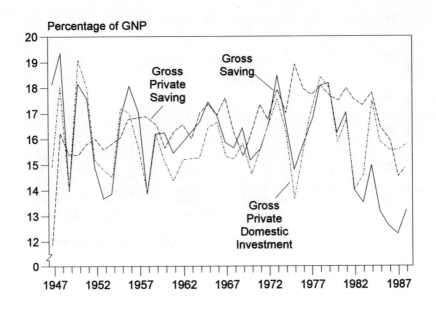

Figure 2.2: **Gross savings and investment**
Source: Economic Report of the President (1989).

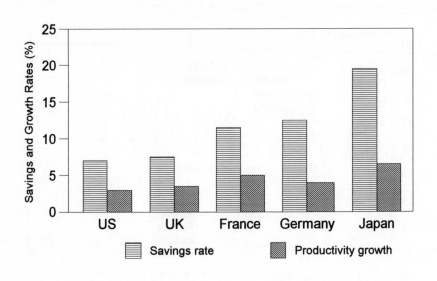

Figure 2.3: **Savings and growth rates 1970-1990**
Source: Harvard Business Review, March-April 1987.

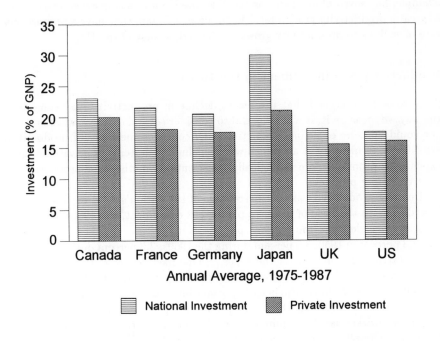

Figure 2.4: **International comparison of gross fixed investment**
Source: Economic Report of the President (1990).

The importance of the savings rate in fuelling economic growth and international competitiveness is apparent when we compare the US's meagre growth rate in savings and productivity to Japan's, depicted in Figure 2.3.

As the deficit grew, the amount of national resources that could be devoted to investment shrunk. In Figure 2.3 we find that the correlation between savings and economic growth is consistent between countries over time. Germany, for example, has saved about twice as much as the US and has enjoyed nearly twice as great a productivity growth rate. In the case of Japan, they have a proportional rate of savings to productivity growth nearly triple that of the US.

Productivity and investment in the 1980s

Since some have argued that the recent decline in productivity may come from the way we measure it, it will be useful to consider several different ways in which one could measure or define productivity. Of course, some types of productivity are difficult to measure at all, which would include such items as private or public expense to promote more ecologically conscientious methods of production, or safer consumer products.

Defining productivity as that percentage of the nation's total income invested in additions to the base of business plants and equipment, the 1980s were worse than any decade since the postwar period. Net business capital formation was about 3 percent in 1950, 3.5 percent during the 1960s, 3.3 percent during the 1970s, and a startling 2.3 percent for the 1980s.[2] One likely cause of this productivity decline was the decline in the growth of capital stock relative to the labour force, or capital intensity. This ratio is an important indicator of productivity, or output per worker, for two reasons. First, the production processes which generate more output per worker usually require more capital per worker; and second, increasing the ratio generally means investing in newer capital. Since this newer capital is more likely to embody more advanced technologies than older capital, it is expected to increase the efficiency of the capital stock.

In 1950, for example, there was $26,000 in plant and equipment behind the average worker in America in current dollars. By 1980 this amount had grown to $43,100 per worker, and today the average worker has only $45,000 worth of equipment behind him or her. In fact, the increase in the rate of capital intensity of production was cut in half during the 1980s.[3] This means that the increase in the amount of capital per labourer has been nearly stagnate: clearly not much of an improvement over a decade ago, before there were tax-based investment incentives in place to stimulate capital formation!

Measures of investment

Why is investment important?

Investment is critical to the economy because new capital is necessary to incorporate technical advances into production. Replacement investment as well as capacity expansion offer the opportunity to install improved equipment and newer technologies. Increasing the gross investment rate allows for faster adoption of innovations, thus raising the quality of the capital stock. It also contributes to overall economic growth or productivity by increasing the total amount of capital available for production.

How do we measure investment?

When people talk about low investment levels in the US, what do they mean? One answer is that they could mean that the US devotes a smaller percentage of its Gross National Product to the purchase of fixed equipment. An international comparison of both the private and national investment percentages between 1975 and 1987 is presented in Figure 2.4.

Figure 2.4 indicates that investment in the US between 1975 and 1987 was low by international standards. Between 1975 and 1987, the US devoted an average of 17.5 percent of the GNP to national investment, while other countries (Canada, France, Germany, Japan and the UK) channelled 22.5 percent of their GNP on average into investment. In fact, the US has the single lowest investment rate in the sample. Even Canada, a neighbour with a similar economic structure in many ways, averaged 22.8 percent investment.

Allowing for an alternative measure to capture the overall picture of US investment of the 1980s, we can examine the real net investment of the US as a percentage of GNP since the 1940s. In Figure 2.5 we have both the fixed non-residential and total fixed rates plotted from 1948 to 1988.

Using this measure as an indicator of overall investment, the situation looks even worse. Defining the Net National Product (NNP) as GNP minus depreciation, it appears that net investment remained below the postwar average during the entire decade of the 1980s. Also it is interesting to note the trend of an increasing gap between the gross and net investment rates over time. This reflects the fact that equipment has risen as a share of total capital stock, which means that the depreciation fraction of the GNP is growing over time.

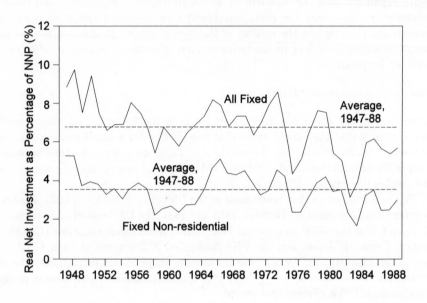

Figure 2.5: **US real net investment as a percentage of NNP**
Source: Department of Commerce.

14

Tax-based incentives and investment

It is clear that any plan to promote productivity or increased capital formation is going to have to consider incentives for the individual and the firm to invest. Theoretically, any tax law change which reduces the marginal cost of investment to the firm will encourage investment. Policy makers at that time outlined three tax measures for affecting firm investment through tax-based incentives: changes in the investment tax credit, changes in the statutory corporate tax rate, and changes in depreciation allowances. The design and impact of these tax code changes will be examined in the next chapter.

Notes

1. See *Economic Report of the President*, US Government, (1986).

2. See *National Income and Product Accounts*, US Department of Commerce, (1959-1988).

3. See Friedman (1988).

3 Tax reform and investment

Introduction to tax reform

This chapter analyzes the tax reforms of the 1980s in terms of the goals of the reforms as outlined by the Reagan administration, as well as the success of the administration in achieving their goals. Preliminary findings in this chapter indicate that the tax reforms were not successful overall in their ability to increase incentives for firms to invest in capital stock. The conclusions of this chapter are supported by empirical evidence presented in Chapters 5 and 6, which explore firm investment behaviour at both the individual and aggregate levels during the 1980s.

Findings of this research also support the hypothesis that the tax reform Acts were also unsuccessful in increasing individual savings, reducing the deficit, or increasing the productivity of the economy. The reasons for these failures are important because they provide lessons for future policy makers. Chapter 7 explores some alternative solutions to capital formation and productivity problems in light of our experience in the 1980s.

Tax reform: reality and rhetoric investigated

Broadly, there are three ways that the tax structure can provide incentives for the firm to invest. First, any tax that decreases the effective price of new capital goods will provide an incentive for the firm to invest. Tax cuts that decrease the effective price on new capital include increases in the Investment Tax Credit (ITC), accelerated depreciation, and depletion allowances. The second way the tax law can provide investment incentives is through cuts in the statutory marginal corporate tax rate. The third would be a decrease in taxes on the returns to investment at the personal level. This would include a reduction in the statutory personal tax rate or a reduction in the capital gains tax. The decade of tax reform started out with the Economic Recovery Tax Act (ERTA) of 1981. This tax legislation introduced measures to encourage firm investment in capital by reducing the tax burden on the firm through such measures as accelerated depreciation allowances and allowing firms to sell unused tax credits. This Act also included measures first proposed by Congressman Jack Kemp and Senator William Roth, which called for an across the board cut in the personal income tax rate. In 1982 the Tax Equity and Financial Responsibility Act (TEFRA) was enacted in an attempt to make the tax law more neutral and improve the raging government deficit by taking back many of the cuts given out in the previous year. In 1984 another similar but less significant tax act was passed as part of the Deficit Reduction Act (DEFRA). Finally, the 1986 Tax Reform Act (TRA) was passed with mixed bag of tax incentive effects for investment. This reform is widely believed to have increased the marginal cost of new investment to the firm. Proponents of the 1981 and 1982 tax reforms argued that these tax cuts would promote economic recovery by providing greater incentives to work and invest. In order to determine incentive effects we must look at the marginal tax rates, that is to say the extra tax incurred on an additional dollar of income.

The Economic Recovery Tax Act of 1981

Specific provisions of the 1981 ERTA included a 23 percent reduction in personal income tax rates, to be conducted in three stages by 1984.[1] After 1985 the tax rate would then be indexed to inflation. This effective increase in the individual's after-tax wage was expected to have a positive impact on the individual's labour supply, inducing him or her to work more hours because more of each marginal dollar earned could be kept. More hours of work translates into more inputs to production and increased productivity. And since labour supply studies have consistently shown that particularly women's labour supply is elastic with respect to tax changes, both number of hours worked and labour force participation by married women were expected to increase sharply. In Table 3.1 we see a comparison of the marginal personal income tax rates for single and married workers by real income from 1979 to 1986 under the Economic Recovery Act of 1981 and previous law. This table indicates that, without the 1981 law, low and middle-income marginal tax rates would have been 30 to 50 percent higher. This increase in the after-tax income was supposed to lead to an increase in personal saving; bacause borrowing became more expensive, causing individuals to postpone present for future consumption through increased saving.

18

Table 3.1
Personal income tax rates before and after the ERTA of 1981

Real Income	(Percent)							
(1979 dollars)	1979	1980	1981[b]	1982	1983	1984	1985	1986
Single:								
$ 10,000								
Old law	21	21	21	24	24	24	24	26
New law	-	-	21	22	19	18	18	18
$ 20,000								
Old law	30	30	34	34	34	34	39	39
New law	-	-	34	31	28	26	26	26
$ 30,000								
Old law	39	39	39	44	44	49	49	49
New law	-	-	39	40	36	38	38	34
$ 50,000								
Old law	49	50	50	50	50	50	50	50
New law	-	-	49	50	45	48	48	48
Married, two workers:								
$ 10,000								
Old law	16	16	18	18	18	18	18	18
New law	-	-	18	16	15	14	14	14
$ 20,000								
Old law	21	24	24	24	28	28	28	28
New law	-	-	24	22	19	22	18	18
$ 30,000[a]								
Old law	28	32	32	32	37	37	37	43
New law	-	-	32	29	26	28	28	28
$ 50,000								
Old law	43	43	43	49	49	49	49	49
New law	-	-	42	44	40	38	38	38

a Excludes social security taxes and State and local income taxes.
b Tax rates for 1981 under new law rounded to nearest whole percent.
Source: Department of Treasury, Office of Tax Analysis.

19

To provide more incentives for the individual to save, the tax code also extended the eligibility for the Individual Retirement Accounts (IRA) and Keogh savings plans. Unfortunately, savings rates did not increase and, as shown in Figure 2.2, rates have been declining on average since the late 1970s. What the administration had not accounted for was the fact that consumers might choose to consume more rather than save more with their higher after-tax incomes. In addition, this decrease in the personal income tax rate provided a disincentive for the firm to retain earnings. This was expected to have a positive impact on firm investment. As we shall see in the next chapter, it is not only possible but important to incorporate this effect of the personal income tax rate into our measure of the cost of capital to the firm.

Another provision of the Act was to provide inflation indexing of tax brackets. Personal exemptions and the zero brackets were all increased by the percentage increase in prices that occurred during the year ending the previous 30th of September. This indexing was to prevent the bracket creep which causes individuals to move into higher tax brackets while their real incomes do not increase.

A substantial speed-up of depreciation deductions used in calculating business taxes was also implemented as part of the tax plan. This Accelerated Cost Recovery System (ACRS) provided a strong incentive for the firm to invest in two ways.

First, it decreased the effective price of new capital goods by allowing firms to write off the cost of equipment more quickly. Second, it increased the after-tax profits of the firm. Specifically, businesses were permitted to write off industrial equipment over an average of 5 years rather than 8.6 years. For industrial plants, asset lives were reduced from 23.8 years to 15 years. The depreciation schedules after 1984 provided increasingly faster depreciation of assets. For certain types of equipment, there was also an investment tax credit offered, to lower the marginal cost to the firm of purchasing certain types of new equipment. The combined impact of ACRS and ITC was to decrease the effective price of new capital goods over the period 1982 to 1987. The effective tax rates on new depreciable assets for various industries are shown in Table 3.2. Under the new law, effective tax rates across industries were cut sharply from old levels; however, some industries were helped more than others. This is because the capital to labour ratio is different across industries, and the tax law applies only to capital inputs, not labour.

For instance, capital-intensive industries like Motor Vehicles were substantially helped by this tax change with a new tax rate of -11.3 from 25.8, compared to Services and Trade with a new rate of 37.1 from 53.2 percent. And while Motor Vehicles industries will not actually be subsidized by transfer payment, this negative rate would result in a lower total corporate tax bill for the firm.

Table 3.2
Effective tax rates for sample industries in 1982

Industry[a,b]	Old Law	New Law
Agriculture	32.7	16.6
Mining	28.4	-3.4
Primary metals	34.0	7.5
Machinery and instruments	38.2	18.6
Motor vehicles	25.8	-11.3
Food	44.1	20.8
Pulp and paper	28.5	9.0
Chemicals	28.8	8.6
Petroleum refining	35.0	1.1
Transportation services	31.0	-2.9
Utilities	43.2	30.6
Communications	39.8	14.1
Services and trade	51.2	17.1

a Industries chosen had at least $5 billion in new investment in 1981.
b Assumes a 4 percent real after-tax rate of return and 8 percent inflation.
Source: Department of the Treasury, Office of Tax Analysis.

The 'Safe-Harbor' leasing provision allowed firms to reduce their tax liabilities through sales of unused tax credits, thereby increasing the firm's after-tax profits. This was also expected to reduce incentives for mergers because, under the old code, companies with high tax liabilities had an incentive to merge with companies which had tax losses. Since the tax credits were transferable, companies with positive taxable income could simply purchase the tax credits of the low-income company without actually merging. Overall, these tax cuts lowered individual income taxes and provided positive incentives for the firm to invest in capital.

But these benefits to the firm came with a price tag. It is estimated that the 1981 tax revisions reduced federal tax revenues by $60 billion during 1981 and 1982, and would have resulted in further reductions of $250 billion during 1983 and 1984 had further revisions of the tax code not taken place. Meyers (1988) concludes that the 1981 and 1982 tax acts had the net effect of cutting federal revenue by a total of $245 billion from what it would have been under the prior law from 1981 to 1984. Further, it is speculated that the real effects of the tax cuts would most likely be undone by continuing bracket creep, rising social security taxes and increasing indirect taxes.

Certainly the 1981 tax code made a significant difference in terms of the tax revenues collected to offset the spending of the federal government. The important question is: did America incur a net benefit from the 1981 tax reform in terms of increased capital formation and productivity? Unfortunately, the answer is probably not. The increased economic activity that the administration had hoped for never happened. From the 1981 budget figures, the administration projected a real economic growth rate of 4.4 percent annually during the 1982 to 1986 period. The economy expanded by about 2.4 percent per annum on average over these five years. This meant that the capital formation that had been hoped for was not realized, or at least not in the envisioned time horizon of the administration's plans.

Further, without cuts in federal spending, the total federal spending share of America's income rose as the tax share of income fell. In 1981 the spending share was 23 percent, with a tax share of 20 percent. By the end of 1982, the spending share was 24 percent, but the tax share had fallen to 18 percent.[2] The problem was that the Reagan administration had grossly overestimated the incentive effects of the lower tax rates at both the individual and firm levels. It further compounded this error by underestimating the differential between tax revenue and federal spending. They also may have counted too heavily on the Fed for support.

The early 1980s were characterized by a tight monetary policy by the Fed in an effort to combat what were perceived as deep-seated inflationary pressures. It was generally accepted that these restraints were necessary in order to restore stable prices, even at the cost of a business downturn.[3] In July of 1982 the

Federal Reserve started to ease monetary policy, and rates began to drop immediately, with Treasury bill rates down to 8 percent by the end of the year. Many economists, including Benjamin Friedman of Harvard University, attributed the ensuing recovery in 1983 and 1984 to the Federal Reserve Chairman Paul Volker's 1982 reversal of monetary policy as much as Reagan's expansionary fiscal policy.

Deeply concerned about the revenue loss and resulting burgeoning deficit, Congress adopted the Tax Equity and Fiscal Responsibility Act of 1982.

The Tax Equity and Fiscal Responsibility Act of 1982

TEFRA 1982 restricted sales of unused tax credits and reduced depreciation allowances by half of any investment tax credit claimed. Both halving the depreciation allowances by ITC claim and curtailing the sales of unused tax credits effectively increased the price of new capital investment. Friedman (1988) estimates that the passage of the 1982 and 1984 tax reforms increased federal tax revenues by $69 billion. While an impressive revision, the federal budget deficit hadn't come within $171 billion of its target. Still plagued by a low capital formation rate and sluggish productivity, Congress passed yet another tax reform, which would turn out to be the most ambitious tax reform in US history.

The 1986 Tax Reform Act

According to the *Economic Report of the President*, the 1986 TRA was to present a broad overhaul of both the personal and corporate taxes in order to eliminate many of the tax preferences that distorted consumption choices and reduced efficiency of resource allocation. The revenues obtained from reducing these wasteful tax preferences were to have allowed a reduction in the statutory marginal tax rates for tax-payers, to provide improved incentives for work and capital formation.[4]

In other words, the basic *ideology* of cutting taxes to improve incentives had not changed. It seems as though the administration's past experience with the 1981 and 1982 Acts had not yet provided any lessons. Still hopeful that cutting taxes would reduce the deficit, the administration pushed the new reform through. Only this time, in spite of their stated purpose of improving investment incentives, the tax code actually included several provisions which directly increased the cost of new capital to the firm, resulting in a net negative impact on capital formation.

Of the most damaging of the provisions on capital formation was the repealment of the investment tax credit. This tax credit, which had been in place almost consistently since 1962 in order to encourage capital formation, was previously equal to 10 percent of qualifying investment structures, primarily those on new machinery and equipment. This single provision of the new tax code, rather than encouraging investment, directly increased the effective marginal tax rate on qualifying new investment across industries, making it more difficult than ever for firms to afford new equipment.

Another provision repealed the accelerated cost recovery system put in place in 1982 to encourage investment. This lengthened the depreciation lifetimes of selected equipment. Previously lives were set at 5 years for most equipment, 3 years for light equipment, and 19 years for business structures. Now most equipment is written off in 7 years, and non-residential structures in 31.5 years.[5]

In addition, the Act called for a reduction in the personal marginal income tax rates, and full taxation of capital gains income for individuals. In other words, capital gains income would now be taxable at the same rate as ordinary personal income rather than being treated favourably as 60 percent excludable from taxable income. The purpose of closing this loophole is unclear, although it is reasonable to expect that this would have a positive, albeit small, impact on total tax revenues collected. On the other hand, it has negative long-term impacts on capital formation. Since owners of a business can receive income in the form of capital gains through the sale of equities in the business, this provision would reduce the return to entrepreneurial activity and incentives for capital formation in the long run.

So where in the 1986 tax reform are the proposed incentives for the firm to invest in capital? The answer is that the only section of the code which appeared to benefit firms was the reduction in the statutory corporate tax rate. Specifically, the plan called for a graduated reduction in the corporate tax rate, which was 46 percent in 1986, to 40 percent by 1987, and for years 1988-1990 the rate was set at 34 percent. The only problem is that this reduction in the tax rate is conferred on all firms making profits, whether they purchase a single machine or not. In fact this untargeted tax break does very little to provide specifically for investment incentives and encourage capital formation. Firms were free to use the additional funds for any purpose, including buying new firms, paying out higher dividends, or just about anything else.

In contrast, the tax increases effected by the repeal of the ITC and the ACRS directly increased the cost of capital to any firm wanting to purchase new equipment -precisely a disincentive to invest!

The breakdown of the sources of the resulting tax revenues are even more shocking. Of the $120 billion increase in corporate tax revenues between 1987 and 1991, $188 billion came from the burden to new capital investment, and the $68 billion difference represents the reduction in taxes owed by firms which already had capital in place.[6]

Further, the tax burden on different types of investment was also shifted in a fashion that favoured such investments as owner-occupied housing and biased investment in such items as equipment. This bias contradicts the administration's claim of not only providing incentives to invest in capital, but of making the tax code more neutral to investment choices. Figure 3.1 provides an industry-level breakdown of the impact of the 1986 TRA on new firm investments.

From Figure 3.1 it is clear that the cost of capital went up across all types of investment, but the relative size of the tax increase across equipment was not equal. The big losers in terms of effective marginal tax increases were firms investing in computers and research equipment, industrial equipment and instruments. Curiously, structures, a type of investment often used as a tax shelter, experienced the smallest tax increase of all. One negative implication for US national productivity is that this bias hurts those industries which are most dependent on, or involved in, high technology applications.[7]

So, while it is true that the reduction in the corporate rate may have helped firms, the repealment of the ITC and the ACRS caused the effective tax rate on new equipment to rise, thus raising the overall tax burden facing new investment. The net impact was an overall increase in the effective tax rate on most equipment of about 20 percent, while shifting the US tax burden from households to businesses.

Debt vs equity financing

The tax reform acts also had an impact on the level of investment through its effect on the financing decisions of the firm. The tax code changes at both the individual and firm levels also influenced the firm's optimal choice of debt-equity financing. Historically, personal income taxes have been in place in the United States since 1913 and, for most of this time, taxes on personal income (τ_y) have been different from taxes on equity income. Taxes on equity income include income in the form of dividends or capital gains (τ_c). Specifically, while dividend income has been taxed the same as regular income, capital gains have been taxed more favourably. From the investor's perspective we can model the firm's optimal financial mix from the following relation:

$$(1 - \tau_y)(1 - \tau_c) <> (1 - \tau_f)$$

where (τ_f) is the statutory corporate tax rate. If the left hand side of the equation is larger than the right hand side, the investor is said to prefer debt financing to equity financing for the firm. If the right hand side is larger than the left hand side, then equity financing is preferred. Note that there is a preference for

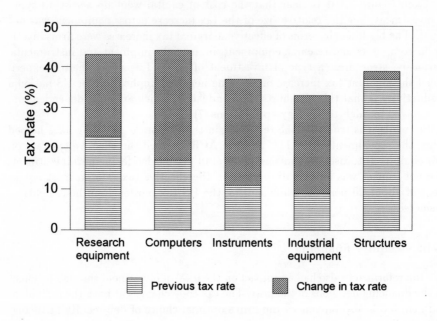

Figure 3.1: **Effective tax rates on corporate investments**
Source: Stephen Meyers (1988).

debt financing whenever there is an increase in the corporate tax rate (τ_f), or there is a decrease in the personal income tax rate (τ_y), or there is an increase in taxes on equity income (τ_c). Of course historically, firms use both (τ_y) types of financing, which Miller suggests is because firms have different 'clienteles' of investors, reflecting the different tax rates faced by individuals in society.[8]

Evidence suggests that, in the presence of imperfect capital markets, the firm's debt-equity decisions are determined in a hierarchical fashion. Studies such as Fazzari, Hubbard and Peterson (1988), which have modelled the cost differential between internal and external funds, find evidence to support the presence of financing hierarchies.[9] Specifically, it has been shown that firms exhibit a hierarchical preference for different types of financing, with internal funds preferred to external funds, and debt financing preferred to equity. Taxes affect the cost of financing through non-debt shields like depreciation and depletion allowances and the ITC. It is also true that non-debt shields can reduce the expected shield benefit of additional debt. This means that the contribution to the value of the firm of an additional unit of debt is not constant but declines with expanded debt usage, because it increases the probability that the debt shields will be redundant for any given amount of non-debt shielding.

The 1981 TRA provided a decrease in the personal income tax, which we would expect to increase investor preference for debt financing of the firm. This tax Act provided further encouragement for debt financing by including a provision for an accelerated cost recovery system. The 1986 TRA increased depreciation lives, reduced the ITC, and eliminated the special treatment of capital gains, all of which supported a debt preference in corporate financing. Calculations in the next chapter indicate that overall there was an increase in the use of debt financing during the 1980s, and particularly after 1984. The higher levels of corporate debt financing has had at least two adverse side effects on the economy.[10]

The first adverse effect evolved from the fact that increases in corporate leverage tend to result in deterioration of the quality of the firm's debt on the margin. One reason for this effect is that the increased leverage simply reduces the capital buffer against default, and thereby increases the risk of a corporation defaulting on its debt. The debt rating agencies, and market response to such an increase in risk is to downgrade the quality assessment or rating of that firm's debt. This is consistent with the recent increases observed in 'junk' debt, that is to say debt that is valued below investment grades. The second adverse effect of a higher level of corporate leveraging is the tendency for this to make the firm more susceptible to adverse changes in income. Thus an unanticipated economic downturn would have a magnified effect on the general economic health of the firm. This is consistent with Bernanke (1983), who warns that the widespread loss of confidence in the liabilities of US corporations could have a depressing systemic effect on economic activity that exceeds the aggregate of the individual losses that firms face.[11]

Conclusions

The findings of this chapter support the hypothesis that, by the end of 1986, the drop in the statutory corporate rate for equity financed investments was outweighed by the reduced value of depreciation allowances and ITCs. In addition, the net effect of the provisions of the 1986 TRA was to increase the tax burden on newly purchased equipment, with a relatively stronger effect on growth in equipment as compared to structures. This hypothesis has been examined by others, with similar conclusions, for example Auerbach and Hassett (1979).[12]

Considering the net impact on the financing decisions of the firm, the reduction of the statutory corporate tax rate lowered the benefits of the interest deduction associated with debt-financed investment, while the reduction in the individual rates and the repeal of the capital gains tax preference shifted the relative costs of equity and debt financing. The net result appears to have been a substantial increase in the use of debt financing in the 1980s.

In addition, many of the stimulatory provisions of the reforms were either paired with negative tax laws, resulting in a net effect that was either weakly negative or weakly positive, or they were immediately revised in the subsequent reform to provide the opposite incentive. In fact, both these types of 'netting out' of investment incentives of various tax code measures were observable in the 1986 TRA, the 1981 ETRA and 1982 TRA respectively. Policy makers of the 1990s also need to keep in mind that, while two particular tax cuts may cost the same in terms of federal revenue loss, they may have very different stimulatory effects on the firm. For instance, if the goal of the reform is to stimulate new investment, it makes much more sense to increase the investment tax credit rather than cut the statutory corporate tax rate.[13]

The ITC or accelerated depreciation stimulate more investment per dollar of tax cut than a more general cut in the statutory corporate tax rate. The reason for this is that the firm is not required to spend the tax savings on increased investment but is free to use funds for other proposes such as increases in retained earnings or dividend payments. This 'bang-for-the-buck' consideration in selecting tax cuts to stimulate investment underscores the message that not all tax cuts are created equal.

Notes

1. See Meyers (1988), pp. 3-16.

2. Ibid.

3. It was because of this tight monetary policy that interest rates reached such peaks in 1980 and 1981.

4. See *Economic Report of the President* (1989), US Government, pp. 87-9.

5. Ibid.

6. See Summers (1987), p. 54.

7. Auerbach and Hassett (1979) study in detail the tax effects on various industries. They find, among other things, that the boon associated with information processing and the decline in petroleum exploration explain much of the significant divergence between the performance of the equipment and structures categories. For a broader discussion, Nelson and Wright (1993) examine the fall of America's technological leadership in the postwar period.

8. See Miller (1977), pp. 261-75.

9. See Fazzari, Hubbard and Peterson (1988), pp. 271-83.

10. See Pozdena (1989), pp. 37-50.

11. See Bernanke (1983), pp. 257-76.

12. According to Auerbach and Hassett, tax factors moved in the opposite direction of investment growth in the post-1986 TRA era. That is to say, the 1986 TRA has not appeared to have played a significant role in explaining the investment patterns in equipment and structures over the past few years. They believe there may be other significant macroeconomic factors which must explain these non-results, such as technological innovation.

13. This study does not attempt to distinguish between stimulation of short-term rather than long-term asset types.

4 The Q theory of investment

Taxes, dividends, and liquidity constraints

In this chapter a Q theory of investment framework is developed to examine the investment behaviour of the firm in the 1980s. This framework will allow us not only to determine what happened to firm level investment, but how and why certain factors affected the firm's incentive to invest. In attempting to estimate the investment behaviour of the firm, it is critical to employ a model that allows us to separate and control for as many of the factors determining investment behaviour as possible.

This framework will allow us to examine the relative importance of dividend policy and liquidity constraints on the firm's decision to invest, as well as incorporate tax reform impacts on firm investment incentives. Unlike previous definitions of Q, the proxy for the firm's marginal cost of investment, this work develops a Q which incorporates the impact of the personal marginal tax rate, which we know should affect the cost of capital to the firm. Further, this work employs a methodology which allows us to directly model the dividend payment of the firm and test for sensitivity of investment to dividend policy specification. This is important because previous empirical Q studies, such as Summers (1981) for example, have assumed a structure for the dividend payment of the firm which is residually determined, rather than actual.

Both theory and results of estimations of the dividend payment show that this alternative specification of the dividend payment of the firm fits the data better. Finally, using this specification, we can then test for the impact of liquidity constraints on firm investment behaviour to determine if the availability of funds to the firm is a good indication of firm investment behaviour. If this is the case, there are important implications for policy makers interested in stimulating the capital formation of the firm.

Historical development of Q theory

The Q theory of investment has its roots in the works of Brainard and Tobin (1968) and Tobin (1969). These works employ Q as a link between the financial and real sectors of the economy, where it is assumed the economy has assets of only money and capital. Mathematically, one can derive Q as the first-order condition of the firm's dynamic optimization problem, relating the firm's marginal costs of adjustment to the shadow price of a unit of capital. Under particular assumptions, this theoretical relationship can be estimated empirically because of the link between the unobservable shadow price of capital and the stock market valuation of existing capital. For purposes of empirical research then, Q can be defined as the ratio of the market value of the firm to the replacement value of the firm's capital stock.[1]

Recently, there has been a renewed interest in empirically testing the Q theory of investment model. This interest is undoubtedly due in part to the availability of panel data sets as much as the increased awareness that this model offers a rich context in which to study firm investment behaviour. For notational clarity we can let Q stand for the tax-adjusted Q and let q denote Tobin's q, or q in a taxless world. In Bishoff (1976) we find the first comparison of the performance of q with other investment models in explaining aggregate corporate investment. In these studies the q equations are out-performed by both the accelerator and neoclassical flexible accelerator equations. Malkiel, Von Furstenberg and Watson (1980) provide the first study examining the effects of q on gross fixed investment at a disaggregated industry level. An important result of their study, which has been disputed, is that changes in q have a greater impact on fixed investment at the industry level than at the aggregated corporate level.[2] The incorporation of a tax bias theory into the q theory framework was introduced by Auerbach in 1979.[3] His work emphasizes that it is because of the differential between taxation of dividends and capital gains that the values of the marginal Q can fall below unity in spite of any future opportunities or monopoly rents available to the firm. This implies that a firm will equate the payment of \$1 to shareholders, which provides the shareholder with $(1 - \tau_y)$ dollars after personal taxes, with reinvestment of one dollar, which would provide the shareholder with a capital gains after personal taxes of $(1 - \tau_c)$ dollars. Under these circumstances, Q will not tend to unity but rather $(1 - \tau_y)$ over $(1 - \tau_c)$. Thus a rational and efficient manager should be willing to spend a dollar to buy capital that is worth less than one dollar under certain tax policies. An underlying assumption of this model, which has been maintained in the ensuing literature, is that the repurchase of equity by the firm is constrained; that is to say, it is assumed that there is no repurchasing of shares by the firm. Auerbach's finding is significant because it illustrates how, in the presence of taxes, our optimality conditions for Q change. Recall, in Tobin's taxless world, firms are willing to invest up to the point where each dollar spent purchasing capital raises the market value of the firm by at least a dollar. In Tobin's model we use Hayashi's (1982) result that the average q is a reasonable proxy for the unobservable marginal q.[4] In a taxless world, q is equal to the value of the firm divided by its capital stock, which can alternatively be defined as the ratio of the market value of firm to its replacement cost. Summers (1981) and Salinger and Summers (1983) outline a methodology for accounting for the effects various tax rates have on estimations of Q. Specifically, they derive the mathematical link between the theoretical model of the firm and an econometric specification in terms of observable parameters. They analyze 30 $Standard and Poor(S\&P)$ firms from 1959-1978, using the dividend policy assumption that dividends are set equal to the after-tax profits of the firms minus the costs of adjustment. One conclusion of their research is that the evolution of investment depends on the depreciation tax-shields attributable to prior investments. Thomas Downs (1990) provides further empirical evidence to support Summer's assertion by showing that a significant proportion of the variation in Q occurs because of differences in accumulated tax depreciation shields. One implication of his work is that erosion of depreciation tax-shields over time can be expected to decrease Q values. There is a rich body of literature which has developed, examining the impact of financial factors on firm investment behaviour. Some of the empirical papers which have sought to test investment sensitivity to liquidity constraints include Fazzari, Hubbard and Peterson (1988), Devereux and Schiantarelli (1989), Oliner and Rudebusch (1989), Elston (1993) and Gilchrist (1989). Using cash flow as a measure of liquidity, these studies conclude that liquidity constraints matter for many firms, including those with low dividend-payout ratios. Specifically, Devereux and Schiantarelli, who explicitly model the agency and financial distress costs for British manufacturing data, conclude that cash flow appears to play a more important role for larger rather than smaller firms. Gilchrist (1989) examines the role of financial and liquidity constraints in investment using both Q theory models and Euler equations on US data. His results indicate that cash flow matters most for financially constrained firms, and provide support for a model based on financing hierarchies that result from imperfect capital markets. Fazzari *et al.* also support a model based on financing hierarchies, but conclude that Q is at best one of the few significant explanatory variables for explaining firm investment. Many of these papers have also used various sorting strategies to examine the cross-sectional differences in the role of liquidity in the Q theory investment model. Hayashi and Inoue (1991), for example, develop a model of investment with multiple capital goods, using panel data from Japanese manufacturing firms sorted by heavy and light manufacturing sectors. One interesting finding of theirs is that adjustment costs were less than half the gross profits net costs of adjustment, based on the Q coefficient.[5] Adjustment costs are those associated with changing capital stock levels, and would include, for example, the cost of unbolting and removing machinery from the factory. Elston (1993) examines bank-affiliated and independent firms in the German manufacturing sector over time. Results indicate that investment sensitivity to liquidity constraints is greater for the independent firms, and that liquidity constraints were relatively non-binding for the large firms with close relationships to banks. Regardless of the sorting strategy used, however, these studies consistently found that liquidity constraints play an important role for firms facing financing constraints. Many of the recent empirical studies have also mentioned the importance of examining the role of dividend behaviour in affecting the cost of capital facing firms. However, these studies either do not address the issue in the empirical work or resort to estimations based on subsets of the data which consist of one set of firms that do pay dividends and another that do not. It is important to note that Devereux and Schiantarelli and Hayashi and Inoue do not attempt to account for differences between firms' dividend payout behaviour. Fazzari *et al.* and Gilchrist both run estimations on subsets of data divided by payout behaviour, but do not model the dividend process explicitly. In fact, while Devereux and Schiantarelli use the former approach, they point out that without explicitly modeling why firms pay dividends it is not clear which firms are constrained by their earnings. This book addresses this issue by explicitly modelling the firm's dividend policy in the definition of Q, which represents the firm's marginal cost of capital investment. This work extends the current literature by developing and employing a methodology which explicitly models the dividend process of the firm in testing the sensitivity of the Q investment model to liquidity constraints. Estimations in the next chapter are performed on a panel of US firms from 1975-1989, subdivided into four groups based on firm size. In general, there are primarily two ways that the firm's dividend policy can be expected to effect investment levels. The first is through the cost of capital, which is directly affected by the definition of the dividend policy rule of the firm. The second is an indirect effect on investment because dividend payments effect the liquidity constraint of the firm, which in turn directly affects the ability of the firm to invest. In this chapter a formal link is developed between the model of the firm within an intertemporal framework and an empirical specification described strictly in terms of observable parameters. This process enables us to empirically estimate and test tax-adjusted Qs which are constructed from balance sheet information of the firm. In order to examine the importance of dividend policy specification, a new tax-adjusted Q, or Q_1, is developed based on the dividend policy rule that firms offer a fixed dividend yield to stock holders on their equity, from Turnovsky (1990).[6] Previous empirical studies in the Q literature have exclusively used a dividend policy rule which defines dividends residually as the tax profits of the firm minus the estimated costs of adjustment.

Theoretically, the new tax-adjusted Q_1 is a more appealing way of describing the complex dividend process of firms than the traditional residual process explanation. This is because a fixed payout level is consistent with known characteristics of firm dividend payout behaviour. One such stylized fact is the well known 'sticky' nature of dividends. That is to say that once firms have set a dividend payout level they attempt to maintain that payout level because large variations may send the wrong signal to investors.[7] Empirically, this dividend policy assumption is validated by estimations of the dividend payment regressed on the value of the firm. We can use both Qs to examine the sensitivity of the Q theory of investment model to dividend policy specification and liquidity constraints.

From a policy perspective, these estimations provide an important source of information on corporate investment behaviour during a decade of frequent tax reform largely dedicated to improving firm incentives to invest in capital. Robert Lucas (1976) points out that, when policy changes, it is an ideal time to study how our econometric models have fared during the period of change. Following the logic of the Lucas Critique, the 1980s are an ideal period to test the relationship between tax effects on Q, and Q's predictive power in explaining corporate investment behaviour.

Development of the Q theory of investment model

Following Brock and Turnovsky (1981) we can model the behaviour of the firm in accordance with the traditional neoclassical production function (F) with the firm using inputs of capital (K) and labour (L). In this model we assume that both marginal products are positive but diminishing such that $F_l > 0$, $F_k > 0$ and $F_{ll} < 0$, $F_{kk} < 0$ and that $F_{kk}F_{ll} - F_{kl}^2 = 0$ where single and double subscripts denote first and second derivatives of the production function with respect to factor inputs. I also assume non-monopoly rents, a constant returns to scale production function with homogeneity of factors, and complementarity of factor inputs such that $F_{kl} = F_{lk} > 0$.

Given these assumptions, we can define the gross profits of the firm as

$$R = F(K, L) - wL \tag{4.1}$$

where (F) is the production function of the firm based on capital (K) and labour (L) inputs, and (w) is the real wage rate, which is determined by the market because the firm is a price taker in this model. If corporate profits are taxed at (τ_f) and the remainder is either paid out as dividends (D) or kept as retained earnings (RE) then the following equation describes corporate sources and uses of funds

$$(1 - \tau_f) R = D + RE. \qquad (4.2)$$

Since equipment requires installation we define a convex cost of adjustment (H) as a function of investment (I) and capital (K) by

$$H \left(\frac{I}{K} \right) K. \qquad (4.3)$$

Costs of adjustment enter the model because firms cannot costlessly and instantly adjust the capital stock; rather, they face costs of equipment installation and removal. Here the marginal cost of adjustment is defined as an increasing function of the rate of investment where H_I, $H_{II} > 0$. This means that, as the firm increases investment, it becomes more costly to do so, that is to say there exist some diseconomies of scale with respect to increases in capital investment. In this model, it is also assumed that there are adjustment costs for capital but not for labour. This construction implies the firm is always able to hire the desired quantity of labour, but will only gradually close the gap between the desired and the actual levels of capital stocks.

The financing constraint facing firms can then be defined as

$$RE + s\dot{E} = (1 - b)H \left(\frac{I}{K} \right) K, \qquad (4.4)$$

where (b) is the fraction of the capital stock of the firm that is maintained as debt, representing bond financing, (s) is the price of an issue, (E) is the outstanding stock of the firm, and (τ_f) is the corporate tax rate. The dot notation above the (E) denotes the time derivative of equity. This equation describes both the sources and uses of funds, and eliminates the need for a discussion on portfolio problems. In the most general case, financing can come from any combination of these three sources. However, for operational simplicity, throughout the remainder of this model I will assume that the firm does not use debt financing such that $b = 0$, nor does it repurchase existing shares. This assumption simplifies the problem, but holds constant any possible effects from monetary policy. The value of outstanding equities (V) can then be described as

$$V = sE. \qquad (4.5)$$

36

Hence prices are proportional to the outstanding value of the firm's equity, and from Equations 4.2 and 4.4 we then derive an expression for dividends of the firm where

$$D = (1 - \tau_f) \left[R - H \left(\frac{I}{K} \right) K \right] + s\dot{E}. \tag{4.6}$$

Combining Equation 4.6 with the consumer optimality condition for equities and the time derivative of Equation 4.5 we can derive the following equation for explaining the evolution of the value of the firm over time:

$$\dot{V} = \frac{\theta}{(1 - \tau_c)} V - \left[(1 - \tau_f) R - H \left(\frac{I}{K} \right) K \right] + \frac{(\tau_y - \tau_c)}{(1 - \tau_c)} D, \tag{4.7}$$

where θ is the real required rate of return on equities, which is adjusted by $(1 - \tau_c)$, the tax rate on capital gains. τ_y is the tax rate on ordinary or personal income. From Equation 4.7 we see that, if $\tau_y \neq \tau_c$, then dividend policy is important to the firm. Note that if dividend policy is related to V, as is the case here, the value of equity, then it will affect the cost of capital to the firm $\frac{\theta}{(1-\tau_c)}$. If, on the other hand, it is directed to the flow of earnings, then it has no effect on the cost of capital, but instead affects the flows being accumulated. This model predicts that, as long as $\tau_y > \tau_c$, as it is assumed here, then it is not optimal for firms to pay dividends. It is noted that in spite of this, firms do pay dividends, and I shall consider two possible alternatives of dividend payment behaviour:

$$(I) \qquad D = V\bar{i}$$

$$(II) \qquad D = (1 - \tau_f) \left[R - H \left(\frac{I}{K} \right) K \right]$$

Rule I implies firms offer a fixed dividend yield to stock holders on their equity, i.e. firms set $\bar{i}$ to some minimum level representing a constrained optimal dividend policy. Note that when dividends are set to some minimum level by the firm this includes the possibility that the firm may choose to set dividends to zero. To empirically investigate the feasibility of this dividend policy rule, we can estimate the following model:

37

$$D_t = B_1 V_t + e_t,$$

where D_t is the dividend payment of the firm, V_t is the value of the firm, and e_t is the error term at time t. The value of firm at time t can be calculated by multiplying the number of outstanding shares of the firm by the closing price of shares of the firm at the end of each year. These estimations were carried out on a sample of seventeen *Standard and Poor (S&P)* firms over a twelve-year period. Results of least- square estimations of dividends D regressed on the value of the firm V are listed in Table 4.1.

Table 4.1
Dividends regressed on the value of the firm

Firm	Model: $Dividends_t = B_1 V_t + e_t$ β_1	t-statistic	r-squared
ACA	0.0307	5.5	0.90
American Brands	0.0390	4.2	0.95
American T and T	0.0342	6.5	0.97
Bethlehem Steel	0.0394	8.3	0.96
Eastman Kodak	0.0482	3.3	0.90
Exxon	0.0348	9.1	0.94
General Electric	0.0474	6.1	0.98
Goodyear Tire	0.0219	6.8	0.98
IBM	0.0291	3.3	0.96
International Paper	0.0328	7.2	0.96
Merck	0.0327	5.2	0.97
3M	0.0175	8.5	0.98
Proctor and Gamble	0.0285	8.6	0.98
Sears	0.0285	10.3	0.96
Texaco	0.0992	8.8	0.86
Union Carbide	0.0853	5.8	0.59
United Technologies	0.2650	5.0	0.98

High r-squared values indicate a good fit of the model to the data, and t-statistics indicate that the coefficient on the value of the firm is consistently significant at the

1 percent level. Overall, the empirical evidence suggests that this dividend policy assumption is not only theoretically appealing, but is in fact a very reasonable way to describe the dividend process of the firm.

Rule II implies the marginal source of investment financing is through RE with dividends being determined residually as the after-tax profits of the firm minus costs of adjustment. This dividend policy definition, used by all previous empirical Q studies, is based on Summers (1981).

Development of the model under dividend policy rule I

Applying dividend policy rule I to Equation 4.7 we derive the dividend policy-specific differential equation:

$$\dot{V_1} = \left[\frac{\theta}{1 - \tau_c} + \bar{i} \left(\frac{\tau_y - \tau_c}{1 - \tau_c} \right) \right] V - (1 - \tau_f) \left[R - H \left(\frac{I}{K} \right) K \right]. \quad (4.8)$$

The firm's objective then is to maximize the initial value of equity, $V(0)$, with respect to the inputs K, L, I. We can rewrite Equation 4.8 in the more generalized form as:

$$\dot{V} = \theta^\star V - \gamma (K, L, I). \quad (4.9)$$

Here we can express the required rate of return on capital as:

$$\theta^\star = \left[\left(\frac{\theta}{1 - \tau_c} \right) + \bar{i} \left(\frac{\tau_y - \tau_c}{1 - \tau_c} \right) \right] \quad (4.10)$$

where $\theta^\star$ represents the rate of return after corporate but before personal income taxes or capital gains taxes. In this case the required rate of return is not the same as the cost of capital, which is typically defined as the value of the marginal physical product of capital. It is important to note that this definition of the rate of return on capital includes the dividend payout $\bar{i}$, based on the value of the firm, which is discounted by the personal tax rate minus the capital gains tax rate over 1 minus the capital gains rate. Integrating Equation 4.9 we can express the firm's maximization as a function of the dividend policy problem over time as:

39

$$\text{Max}_{K,L,I} V(0) = \int_t^\infty (1 - \tau_f) \left[R - H\left(\frac{I}{K}\right) K \right] e^{-\int_t^s \theta^\star du} ds \qquad (4.11)$$

s.t.

$$\dot{K}(s) = I(s) - \delta K(s) \qquad (4.12)$$
$$K(0) = K_0. \qquad (4.13)$$

Equation 4.11 suggests that the firm wishes to maximize the net present value of net revenues after taxes by choosing optimal capital, labour and investment levels subject to capital constraints. The first constraint, (s), describes the capital accumulation path whereby the firm invests to replace a deteriorating proportional constant δ of the existing capital stock, K. $K(0)$ is simply the initial capital stock level. At each point in time t then, the firm picks L_t and K_t to maximize the value of the firm V_t, while the optimal value of investment, I_t, is determined residually from the capital accumulation identity. If we assume expectations about future dividend payments of the firm are formed with perfect foresight we can impose the following transversality condition to guarantee a unique solution to our maximization problem:

$$\lim_{s \to \infty} V(s) e^{-\int_t^s \theta^\star du} = 0$$

Rewriting Equation 4.11 in terms of observable parameters, the value of the firm in time t can be expressed:

$$V_{1t} = \int_t^\infty \left[(F(K_t, L_t) - wL)(1 - \tau_f) - \right.$$

$$\left. \left(1 - ITC_t - Z_t + (1 - \tau_f) H\left(\frac{I_t}{K_t}\right) K_t\right) I_t \right] e^{-\int_t^s \theta^\star du} ds + B_t$$

$$(4.14)$$

where K_t and L_t are factor inputs and wL_t is the labour expense, all of which is adjusted by the statutory corporate tax rate, τ_f. The next part of the expression

40

represents the investment expenses, where ITC_t is the investment tax credit, Z_t is the present value of depreciation allowances, and $(1 - \tau_f) H \left(\frac{I_t}{K_t} \right) K_t$ is the net convex costs of adjustment times the capital stock, all of which is multiplied by investment, I_t. All of this is then discounted by θ^*, the real required rate of return on capital. B_t is the present value of depreciation allowances on existing capital stock. Of course, in maximizing Equation 4.14, B_t becomes irrelevant to the firm because it is independent of any current or future decisions.

Tax parameters in Equation 4.14, are allowed to change over time and can be defined as:

$$B(t) = \int_t^\infty \tau_f \delta^T e^{-\delta^T (s-t)} \mu(s) K_t ds \qquad (4.15)$$

$$Z(t) = \int_t^\infty \tau_f \delta^T e^{-\delta^T (u-s)} \frac{\mu(u)}{\mu(s)} du \qquad (4.16)$$

$$\mu(s) = e^{-\int_0^s \theta^* du}. \qquad (4.17)$$

Here, $B(t)$ is the present value of depreciation allowances on existing capital stock, which is a function of the corporate tax rate, τ_f, times the statutory depreciation rate on capital δ^T, discounted by the tax-adjusted required rate of return on capital, θ^*, times the capital stock, K_t. $Z(t)$, the present value of depreciation allowances on new investment is a function of the corporate tax rate, τ_f, times the statutory depreciation rate on capital, δ^T, discounted by the tax-adjusted required rate of return on capital. $\mu(s)$ defines the discount factor, which is derived from the consumer optimality conditions for equity. As defined in Equation 4.17, it is a function of the required rate of return on capital after corporate but before personal income taxes and capital gains taxes. Empirical estimations used the real rate of interest to proxy for the required rate of return on capital. Other details on the construction of the various tax parameters are discussed in Appendix B. Equation 4.14 can then be interpreted as the market value of the firm's equity at time t, which is equal to the after-tax profits of the firm minus investment expenses adjusted for tax and depreciation allowances. Note that all of these variables have been specified in real terms so that there is no need to adjust for price levels. Choice variables such as K_t, L_t, and I_t have time subscripts to reflect the fact that they are chosen in each time period to maximize the value of the firm. Tax variables are of course allowed to change over time, and are also time-subscripted accordingly. The fact that the production function F, and the wage,

w, are not a function of time reflects the model, assumption that technology is constant and that firms have static expectations.

Maximizing Equation 4.14 subject to the capital constraints allows us to derive the following optimality conditions for the firm:

$$F_L = w \tag{4.18}$$

$$[1 - ITC_t - Z_t - b] + (1 - \tau_f) \left[H\left(\frac{I_t}{K_t}\right) K_t + H'\left(\frac{I_t}{K_t}\right) I_t \right] = \lambda_t \tag{4.19}$$

$$(1 - \tau_f) F_k - \left[H\left(\frac{I_t}{K_t}\right) + H'\left(\frac{I_t}{K_t}\right) \frac{I_t}{K_t} \right] (1 - \tau_f) I_t =$$
$$-\dot{\lambda}_t + \lambda_t \left[\theta_t^\star\right]. \tag{4.20}$$

Equation 4.18 suggests that the firm will hire labour until the marginal product of labour is equal to the wage. Equation 4.19 characterizes the investment function. It defines a function which links investment to the shadow price of capital, λ_t, to the tax parameters, and the convex costs of adjustment. Intuitively, the right hand side can be interpreted as the shadow price of an additional unit of capital goods, which should be equal to their marginal cost in after-tax profits on the left hand side of the equation. Equation 4.20 describes the evolution of the shadow price of capital. It guarantees that the shadow price, λ_t, equals the present value of future marginal products of a unit of capital. The condition for zero investment suggests that Equation 4.19 becomes:

$$\lambda_t = [1 - ITC_t - Z_t]. \tag{4.21}$$

Development of the model under dividend policy rule II

Under dividend policy II, where we define the dividend process as $D = (1 - \tau_f) \left[R - H\left(\frac{I}{K}\right) K \right]$, we can define Q_2 using a similar set of procedures but with an alternative set of model assumptions, retracing our steps from Equation 4.7. To simplify this process, this section will focus only on the development of the key equations for Q which are affected by the differing behavioural and dividend policy assumptions of the firm. A complete derivation starting from Equation 4.7 is detailed in Appendix A. Starting with the financing constraint of the firm, if we allow for debt financing but assume that the firm neither issues new equity nor repurchases existing shares, then the constraint contains a $b > 0$:

$$RE + s\dot{E} = (1 - pb)H\left(\frac{I}{K}\right), \tag{4.22}$$

where b is again the fraction of the capital stock maintained as debt, representing bond financing, p is the current price level, s is the price of an issue, E is the outstanding stock of the firm, τ_f is the corporate tax rate, and $H\left(\frac{I}{K}\right)K$ is the convex costs of adjustment. For notational simplicity we can define $C\left(\frac{I}{K}\right) = (1 - pb)H\left(\frac{I}{K}\right)K$ for the ensuing model development.

Under this dividend policy assumption, the definition of the cost of capital, $\theta^\star$, is a function of the real rate of return on equities adjusted for the capital gains tax only. This means that the dividend payout does not affect the cost of capital facing the firm, and we define:

$$\theta^\star = \left(\frac{\theta}{1 - \tau_c}\right).$$

The value of the firm under dividend policy rule II can then be specified in terms of real observable parameters as:

$$V_{2t} = \int_t^\infty \left[(F(K_t, L_t) - wL - bK_t r)(1 - \tau_f) - \right.$$

$$\left. \left(1 - ITC_t - Z_t - b + (1 - \tau_f)C\left(\frac{I_t}{K_t}\right)\right)I_t \right] \left(\frac{1 - \tau_d}{1 - \tau_c}\right) e^{-\int_t^s \theta^\star du} ds + B_t \tag{4.23}$$

where K_t and L_t are factor inputs, wL_t is the labour expense, and rbK_t is the expensed interest on the debt, all of which is adjusted by the statutory corporate tax rate, τ_f.[8] The next part of the expression represents the investment expenses, where ITC_t is the investment tax credit, Z_t is the present value of depreciation allowances, b is the fraction of the capital that the firm maintains as debt, and $(1 - \tau_f) C \left(\frac{I_t}{K_t} \right)$ is the net convex costs of adjustment, all of which is multiplied by investment, I_t. Consistent with Summers, this model does not multiply the convex costs of adjustment by the capital stock in the investment expense equation. This specification also implies that the firm will expense interest payments on its debt, which will reduce the after-tax profits of the firm in the model. This model also expenses the adjustment costs of the firm, making them ineligible for investment tax credit. All of this is then discounted by $\left(\frac{1-\tau_d}{1-\tau_c} \right)$ times $\theta^\star$, the real required rate of return on capital. B_t is the present value of depreciation allowances on existing capital stock. Again in maximizing Equation 4.23 B_t becomes irrelevant to the firm because it is independent of any current or future decisions. Tax parameters are allowed to change over time and are defined similarly to Equations 4.15-4.17 with differences detailed in Appendix A. Equation 4.23 can then be interpreted as the market value of the firm's equity at time t under dividend policy II, which is equal to the after-tax profits of the firm minus investment expenses adjusted for tax and depreciation allowances. Maximizing this equation subject to the capital constraints allows us to derive the following optimality conditions for the firm:

$$F_L = w \tag{4.24}$$

$$(1 - ITC_t - Z_t - b) + (1 - \tau_f) \left[C \left(\frac{I_t}{K_t} \right) + C' \left(\frac{I_t}{K_t} \right) \frac{I_t}{K_t} \right] =$$
$$\lambda_t \left(\frac{1 - \tau_c}{1 - \tau_d} \right) \tag{4.25}$$

$$\left[(1 - \tau_f)(F_k - br) - \left(\frac{I_t}{K_t} \right)^2 C' \left(\frac{I_t}{K_t} \right) (1 - \tau_f) \right] =$$
$$\left[-\dot{\lambda}_t + \lambda_t (\theta_t^\star) \right] \left(\frac{1 - \tau_c}{1 - \tau_d} \right). \tag{4.26}$$

Equation 4.24 suggests that the firm will hire labour until the marginal product of labour is equal to the wage. Equation 4.25 characterizes the investment function which links investment to the shadow price of capital λ_t, the tax parameters and the convex costs of adjustment. Intuitively, the right hand side can be interpreted as the shadow price of an additional unit of capital goods, which should be equal to their marginal cost in after-tax profits on the left hand side of the equation. Equation 4.26 describes the evolution of the shadow price of capital. It guarantees that the shadow price, λ_t, equals the present value of future marginal products of a unit of capital. The condition for zero investment suggests that Equation 4.25 becomes:

$$\lambda_t = \left(\frac{1 - \tau_d}{1 - \tau_c}\right)[1 - ITC_t - Z_t - b].\tag{4.27}$$

Derivation of the empirical Q

Because we have a constant returns to scale production technology and homogeneity of the adjustment cost function by definition, then we can derive our empirical Q as follows. From Hayashi (1982) we have:

$$V_t^\star - B_t = \gamma K_t\tag{4.28}$$

where $V_t^\star$ is the stock market value of the firm when the optimal path is followed, B_t is the value of depreciation allowances, which is equal to γK_t, which is a fixed proportion of the initial capital stock. The maximum principle implies then that

$$\lambda_t = \frac{dV_t^\star}{dK_t}\tag{4.29}$$

where λ_t is the shadow price of new investment or marginal Q.

Combining Equations 4.28 and 4.29 we get:

$$\lambda_t = \frac{V_t^\star - B_t}{K_t}.\tag{4.30}$$

Combining Equations 4.19, 4.21, and 4.30 based on dividend policy I, we can derive our tax adjusted Q_1 in terms of observable parameters as:

$$Q_1 = h\left[\frac{\left(\frac{V_t - B_t}{K_t}\right) - 1 + ITC_t + Z_t}{1 - \tau_f}\right]\tag{4.31}$$

45

where

$$h(Q_1) = \left[H\left(\frac{I_t}{K_t}\right) K_t + H'\left(\frac{I_t}{K_t}\right) I_t \right]^{-1}.$$

Combining Equations 4.25, 4.27, and 4.30 based on dividend policy II, we can derive our tax adjusted Q_2 in terms of observable parameters as:

$$Q_2 = h \left[\frac{\left(\frac{V_t - B_t}{K_t}\right)\left(\frac{1-\tau_d}{1-\tau_c}\right) - 1 + ITC_t + Z_t + b}{1 - \tau_f} \right] \qquad (4.32)$$

where

$$h(Q_2) = \left[H\left(\frac{I_t}{K_t}\right) K_t + H'\left(\frac{I_t}{K_t}\right) I_t \right]^{-1}.$$

Glossary

R = Gross corporate profits of the firm

$F(K, L)$ = Production function for the firm

I = Real investment

K = Real capital

w = Real wages

L = Labour

RE = Retained earnings

V = Value of the firm based on the value of outstanding equities

D = Dividends

θ = Required rate of return on investment

$\theta^{\star}$ = Net required rate of return on investment

s = Price of equities

E = Outstanding stock of the firm

b = Share b of all new investment from debt issues

$\bar{i}$ = Fixed dividend payout level of the firm

H = Convex cost of adjustment

$C = H(1 - b)$

p = Output price

τ_c = Capital gains tax

τ_d = Dividend tax

τ_y = Personal income tax

τ_f = Corporate income tax

ITC = Investment tax credit

δ = Proportional constant of existing capital stock

δ^R = Real rate of depreciation allowance

δ^T = Statutory rate of depreciation

q = Ratio of the market value of the firm to replacement cost of the firm

Q = Tax-adjusted q

Q_1 = Tax-adjusted q under dividend policy assumption I

Q_2 = Tax-adjusted q under dividend policy assumption II

Notes

1. While this definition of Q is standard in the Q literature, it is recognized that this definition relies on accounting data from the firm, which is likely to introduce some amount of bias in the estimation of economic relationships.

2. See Chappel and Cheng (1982), p. 231.

3. See Auerbach (1979), pp. 433-46.

4. See Hayashi (1982), pp. 213-24.

5. See Hayashi and Inoue (1991), pp. 1-35.

6. See Turnovsky (1990) for a complete development of all the consumer optimality conditions. Here we make use of the condition for equities:

$$\theta = (1 - \tau_y)\left(\frac{D}{sE}\right) + (1 - \tau_c) - \left(\frac{\dot{s}}{s}\right), \qquad (4.33)$$

where τ_y is the personal income tax rate and θ is the real rate of return on equities. This condition states that, at the margin, the rate of return on holding equities should be equal to the rate of return on dividends taxed at the ordinary income tax rate, τ_y, plus capital gains taxed at the capital gains tax rate, τ_c.

7. Lintner concluded that the consistency of the dividend payment was important to managers for a variety of reasons, including a sense of prudence, fairness and fear of adverse stock holder reactions.

8. Summers (1981) uses nominal terms, and the derivation in Appendix A is consistent with this representation. Here a real representation is used in order to be consistent with the model developed in this section.

5 A cross-sectional analysis of firm investment

Measuring firm investment incentives

The Q theory of investment framework outlined in Chapter 4 provides the theoretical basis for linking the effects of tax code changes to firm investment decisions. This chapter will develop a procedure for empirically testing this link. Specifically, by calculating Q, our measure of the marginal incentive for the firm to invest, we can estimate a time series of tax-adjusted Qs to examine changes in incentives to invest at the firm level over time.[1]

For this we can employ the observable average Q as a proxy for marginal Q, which is unobservable. Q theory tells us that if a firm exhibits a Q value of less than 1 then there is no incentive for the firm to invest at the margin. Conversely, a Q value greater than 1, indicates a firm has more than a dollar to gain from a dollar of capital investment, indicating an incentive for the firm to invest; and in the steady state the firm exhibits a Q value equal to 1.

We can examine the effectiveness of tax reform incentives on firm investment incentives in the eighties by estimating Q_2 values in 1978 and 1988 for comparison, using seventeen $(S\&P)$ firms. If the tax reforms of the 1980s resulted in an increase in the marginal incentive for the firm to invest, then we would expect higher tax-adjusted Qs in the 1980s than the 1970s.

In order to examine the possible affects of dividend policy assumptions on the Q theory of investment model performance, the model is estimated for each firm under both dividend policy specifications. Results indicate that estimations of the investment equation support the Q theory of investment model under both dividend policy specifications. This is evidenced by the statistical significance of the overall investment equation, as well as the statistical significance of the tax-adjusted Q in effecting investment growth. Further, positive coefficients on Q_1 and Q_2 for most firms support a correlative interpretation of Q with investment.

When testing for policy impacts on investment behaviour, it is important to examine the aggregate levels as well as the impact on individual firm investment. The former is important because the goal of the policy is at a macroeconomic level, that is to say the goal is to increase investment of all firms, not just a single firm. Yet, without examining the individual firm, we are looking at the average effect rather than the actual impact of tax policy on firm investment behaviour. So, in terms of examining the effectiveness of a particular tax reform in increasing investment, it is critical to examine the individual firm response. Therefore this study examines firm investment behaviour at both the firm and aggregate levels examining data as a time series, a cross-sectional sample, and as both simultaneously, so as to obtain the maximum amount of information about the data set of firms as is statistically possible.

Estimation of the investment equation

From Chapter 4 we can define the tax-adjusted Q under dividend policy I, where $D = V\bar{i}$, as:

$$Q_{1t} = \left[\frac{\left(\frac{V_t - B_t}{K_t}\right) - 1 + ITC_t + Z_t}{1 - \tau_f} \right].$$ (5.1)

Alternatively, if we choose to specify a model where costs of adjustments enter the model as a cost of investment rather than being expensed, then we find that the statutory corporate tax rate, τ_f, does not enter our specification of Q, and under dividend policy I we can define:[2]

$$Q'_{1t} = \left[\left(\frac{V_t - B_t}{K_t}\right) - 1 + ITC_t + Z_t \right].$$ (5.2)

Under dividend policy II, where $D = (1 - \tau_f)\left[R - C\left(\frac{I}{K}\right)\right]$, we have:

$$Q_{2t} = \left[\frac{\frac{(V_t - B_t)(1 - \tau_c)}{K_t(1 - \tau_d)} - 1 + ITC_t + Z_t}{1 - \tau_f} \right].$$ (5.3)

Within the context of this model we can specify Tobin's q, or q in a taxless world, as:

$$q_t = \left(\frac{V_t}{K_t} \right). \tag{5.4}$$

The definition of Q_{2t} has an additional discount factor, $\left(\frac{1-\tau_c}{1-\tau_d} \right)$, which does not show up in Q_1. This term is important because as long as $(\tau_d > \tau_c)$ this term will increase the value of the tax-adjusted Q_2. If $\tau_c = \tau_d$ then the discount factor becomes a ratio equal to 1 and does not affect Q. This does not necessarily mean, however, that the two tax-adjusted Qs will converge, because the cost of capital which impacts Q through Z_t and B_t are not the same for Q_1 and Q_2.
Q'_{1t} differs from Q_{1t} only by a factor of $(1 - \tau_f)^{-1}$. This means that decreases in the statutory corporate tax rate can be expected to lower Q_{1t}, while Q'_{1t} would remain unaffected by such changes in the tax code.

We can estimate the general form of the investment function as follows:

$$\frac{I_t}{K_t} = h\left(Q_{it}\right) = \beta_0 + \beta_1 Q_{it} + u_t \tag{5.5}$$

where β_0 is the regression constant, β_1 is the coefficient on Q_{it} under dividend policy i for time t, and u_t is the error term in time t.

In order to use this theoretical framework to examine the response of investment to tax policy changes, we must first be clear on the relation between investment and our tax-adjusted Q. This relation can be interpreted as tracing the economy's adjustment costs schedule for new investments. As the value of Q rises, firms seek to increase their investment until they are just indifferent between installing an extra unit of capital and paying out its cost in the form of increased investment.

For simplicity's sake we can assume that adjustment is costless until some level of investment is reached, and then marginal adjustment costs rise linearly with investment. This implies a linear relationship between the ratio of investment to capital stock and Q, and thus the relation between investment and Q can be estimated via Equation 5.5. This allows us to answer the question: are changes in investment growth correlated with changes in the tax-adjusted Q? If this is the case, we will expect to see the same sign on investment growth as the β_1 coefficient on Q_{it}.

53

It is also important to note that these estimations are not necessarily intended to provide the best possible explanation for investment behaviour. We could, for instance, consider adding other variables to the model in an attempt to improve the fit of the model to the data. However, adding other variables would render a different interpretation of the coefficient on Q, which is currently interpreted as a measure of marginal adjustment costs. In addition, it is recognized that Q is not a wholly exogenous variable for the firm; this and other related econometric issues will be addressed explicitly in Chapter 6.

Empirical results for 17 *S&P* firms

The data used in estimations consisted of 20 years of balance sheet information from 1970-1989 for 17 firms from the *COMPUSTAT II* database. The firms in the study were chosen to update estimated Q_2 values for the same firms reported in Summers (1981).[3] The data is deflated using 1982 as a base year. Details on the derivation of the variables used to estimate Q investment equation are discussed in Appendix B.

Estimation of Tobin's q and Q_2 for 17 firms: 1978 and 1988

Updating Summers (1981), both q and Q_2 are estimated for 1988 and compared with the results published on q and Q_2 for 1978. Figures 5.1, 5.2, 5.3, and 5.4 plot q and Q_2 for 1978 and 1988 for comparison.

In Figure 5.1 we see the tax-adjusted Q_2 and Tobin's q plotted for 1978. The dashed line on the graph at 1 indicates the steady-state value of Q. While both series move together in general, the gap between them suggests that it is important to consider the tax-adjusted Q for studies of investment behaviour. These two series from Summers (1981) indicate that 8 or about half of the firms, have tax-adjusted Q_2 values below unity; indicating a situation were the firm has no incentive to invest at the margin. Remember any Q value less than 1 denotes a firm with a incentive to disinvest. Negative Q values are only possible in the tax-adjusted case and can also be interpreted as a situation where the firm has no incentive to invest.[4] Historically, we note that firms with no incentives to invest may still do so. Figure 5.2 plots the updated Q_2 and q for 1988. The gap between q and the tax-adjusted Q_2 appears to have shrunk since 1978 for nearly all the firms in the study. This would be consistent with the hypothesis that the tax reforms had very little affect, if any, in providing incentives for the firm to invest. Examining results for individual firms in the study for 1988 we find that only 3 firms had Q_2 values less than 1. While the total is fewer than that in 1978, many of the firms experienced decreases in values that did not actually drop below 1.

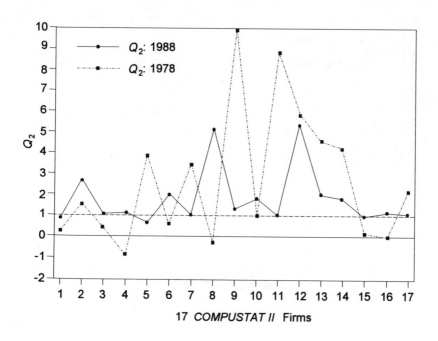

Figure 5.3: Tax-adjusted Q_2 for 17 firms 1978 and 1988

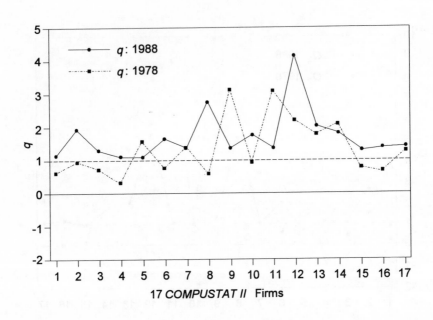

Figure 5.4: **Tobin's** q **for 17 firms 1978 and 1988**

Examining Figure 5.3 which plots the tax-adjusted Q_2 for 1978 and 1988 we find that 8 of the firms experienced a decrease in Q_2 from 1978 to 1988, while the other 9 had higher Q_2 values in 1988 than 1978. This implies that there was an uneven effect on the firms between the two periods, and we cannot say that firms experienced a unilateral improvement in investment incentives as measured by the tax-adjusted Q_2.

Finally Figure 5.4 plots Tobin's q for 1978 and 1988. Here we find clear signals regarding changes in q values over time. That is 12 firms experienced increases in q values over the decade of the study, and no q values were less than 1 in 1988. However, since this does not measure the tax-adjusted incentives to invest, we can infer that the tax adjustments, the only difference between Q and q, are the reason that any of the Q values are less than 1. This supports the hypothesis that the net impact of the tax reforms may have increased the marginal cost of investment for some of the firms in the study.

Comparing q, Q_1, Q'_1 and Q_2 investment model estimations for 1970-1989

Estimating Equation 5.5 for each of these firms for the period 1970 to 1989 will allow us to see how the Q theory model performed in relating changes in Q to investment growth over time. By estimating the investment model for each firm using the tax-adjusted Qs as well as Tobin's q, we can determine if there is empirical evidence to support the hypothesis that tax effects are important in explaining firm investment behaviour.

Tables 5.2, 5.3, 5.4 and 5.5 show investment parameter estimates for q, Q_1, Q'_1, and Q_2 for the 17 firms averaged over 1970-1989. Since all the models had Durbin-Watson values indicating a first-order serial correlation problem, estimates listed in these tables were adjusted using a Cochrane-Orcutt corrective procedure.[5] In Table 5.2, 13 of the 17 firms had R^2 values indicating that at least 60 percent of the variation in investment could be explained by variation in the Tobin's q. In addition, 15 of the 17 firms had t-values for the β_1 coefficients which were significant at the 5 percent level. In Table 5.3, 12 of the 17 firms had R^2 values indicating that at least 60 percent of the variation in investment could be explained by variation in the tax-adjusted Q_1. In addition, 13 of the 17 firms had t-values for the β_1 coefficients which were significant at the 5 percent level.

In Table 5.4, 13 of the 17 firms had R^2 values indicating that at least 60 percent of the variation in investment could be explained by variation in the tax adjusted Q'_1. In addition, 13 of the 17 firms had t-values for the β_1 coefficients which were significant at the 5 percent level.

Looking at estimation results for Q_2 listed in Table 5.5 we see that 12 of the firms had R^2 values in excess of 0.60, and that 12 of the t-values on the β_1 coefficient were significant at the 5 percent level.

In general then, R^2 and t-values are consistent with a good fit of the model to the data supporting the Q theory of investment model under both dividend policy specifications as well as with Tobin's q. Considering the interpretation of these models as a measure of the correlation of Q with investment between the sets of estimates, there is no real difference. Specifically, theory predicts that decreases in the marginal cost of investment should result in increased investment, which implies that the sign of the β_1 coefficient would be positive, consistent with the positive sign on investment. The sign of the β_1 is positive for 15 firms when Tobin's q or Q_1' is used, 14 firms in regressions using Q_1, and 13 firms using Q_2 under dividend policy II. Taken together, these results provide general support for the correlative interpretation of the investment regression. Curiously, these results do not indicate superior explanatory power of using a tax-adjusted Q vs a non-tax-adjusted q to explain changes in investment levels.

Table 5.2
Estimation of the investment model in a taxless world

Model: $\frac{I}{K} = \beta_0 + \beta_1 q + e_t$ t-statistic below			
Firm	β_0	β_1	R^2
ACA	-0.0007	0.0016	0.71
	-1.0 3	2.58	
American Brands	0.0147	-0.0041	0.24
	6.18	-2.48	
American T and T	-0.0056	0.0083	0.85
	-1.56	3.38	
Bethlehem Steel	0.0093	0.0070	0.91
	1.53	2.52	
Eastman Kodak	-0.0065	0.01388	0.70
	-2.96	6.37	
Exxon	0.0026	0.0037	0.80
	1.59	5.23	
General Electric	-0.0043	0.0051	0.79
	-2.40	3.95	
Goodyear Tire	0.0010	0.0042	0.56
	0.23	1.95	
IBM	-0.0095	0.0274	0.62
	-1.01	3.38	

Table 5.2 (continued)
Estimation of the investment model in a taxless world

Model: $\frac{I}{K} = \beta_0 + \beta_1 q + e_t$ t-statistic below			
Firm	β_0	β_1	R^2
International Paper	-0.0034	0.0047	0.41
	-0.92	2.79	
Merck	-0.0329	0.0484	0.71
	-1.95	3.62	
3M	-0.0177	0.0314	0.82
	-0.61	5.23	
Proctor and Gamble	0.0152	0.0167	0.77
	1.02	2.65	
Sears	0.0155	0.0138	0.81
	1.29	2.48	
Texaco	0.0076	0.0026	0.86
	1.78	0.78	
Union Carbide	-0.0117	0.0336	0.73
	-0.72	3.6	
United Technologies	0.3903	-0.2524	0.51
	3.41	-2.66	

Table 5.3
Estimation of investment model under dividend policy I

Model: $\frac{I}{K} = \beta_0 + \beta_1 Q_1 + e_t$ t-statistic below			
Firm	β_0	β_1	R^2
ACA	0.0006	0.0006	0.71
	2.82	2.51	
American Brands	0.0104	-0.0009	0.16
	7.45	-1.18	
American T and T	0.0011	0.0036	0.77
	0.48	2.53	
Bethlehem Steel	0.0203	0.0064	0.89
	5.21	5.02	
Eastman Kodak	0.0053	0.0040	0.70
	13.6	6.22	
Exxon	0.0058	0.0018	0.80
	4.29	5.23	
General Electric	-0.0004	0.0025	0.78
	-0.41	3.66	
Goodyear Tire	0.0058	0.0012	0.52
	2.10	1.44	
IBM	0.0139	0.0088	0.58
	4.08	3.03	

Table 5.3 (continued)
Estimation of investment model under dividend policy I

Model: $\frac{I}{K} = \beta_0 + \beta_1 Q_1 + e_t$ t-statistic below			
Firm	β_0	β_1	R^2
International Paper	-0.0003	0.0025	0.43
	-0.09	2.97	
Merck	0.0086	0.0184	0.74
	1.22	4.24	
3M	0.0118	0.0165	0.84
	0.49	5.81	
Proctor and Gamble	0.0270	0.0090	0.75
	2.56	2.77	
Sears	0.0286	0.0062	0.84
	3.46	2.48	
Texaco	0.0110	-0.0003	0.86
	6.18	-0.25	
Union Carbide	0.0154	0.0143	0.79
	3.05	3.6	
United Technologies	0.1236	-0.0354	0.47
	3.12	-1.09	

Table 5.4
Estimation of investment model under dividend policy I

Model: $\frac{I}{K} = \beta_0 + \beta_1 Q'_1 + e_t$ t-statistic below			
Firm	β_0	β_1	R^2
ACA	0.0009	0.0010	0.70
	8.9	2.2	
American Brands	0.0102	-0.0021	0.21
	11.9	-1.8	
American T and T	0.0039	0.0048	0.78
	2.18	1.56	
Bethlehem Steel	0.0093	0.0070	0.91
	1.53	2.52	
Eastman Kodak	0.0075	0.0072	0.79
	38.4	6.13	
Exxon	0.0066	0.0033	0.80
	4.18	4.8	
General Electric	0.0012	0.0042	0.72
	1.67	2.67	
Goodyear Tire	0.0077	0.0010	0.47
	0.3.2	0.71	
IBM	0.0198	0.0105	0.42
	7.96	1.69	

Table 5.4 (continued)
Estimation of investment model under dividend policy I

Model: $\frac{I}{K} = \beta_0 + \beta_1 Q_1' + e_t$			
t-statistic below			
Firm	β_0	β_1	R^2
International Paper	0.0012	0.0045	0.38
	0.52	2.49	
Merck	0.0186	0.0318	0.69
	3.19	3.58	
3M	0.0174	0.0301	0.82
	0.66	5.4	
Proctor and Gamble	0.0361	0.0133	0.76
	3.72	2.11	
Sears	0.0322	0.0107	0.87
	3.82	2.56	
Texaco	0.0182	0.0035	0.91
	3.49	1.55	
Union Carbide	0.0109	-0.0011	0.84
	8.18	-0.45	
United Technologies	0.0223	0.0256	0.78
	5.82	3.38	

Table 5.5
Estimation of investment model under dividend policy II

Model: $\frac{I}{K} = \beta_0 + \beta_1 Q_2 + e_t$ t-statistic below			
Firm	β_0	β_1	R^2
ACA	0.0012	-1.4600	0.49
	13.8	-0.98	
American Brands	0.0076	0.0043	0.78
	9.06	6.60	
American T and T	0.0041	0.0033	0.90
	4.12	2.30	
Bethlehem Steel	0.0148	0.0053	0.92
	5.35	7.12	
Eastman Kodak	0.0158	0.0083	0.45
	6.95	3.85	
Exxon	0.0081	0.0022	0.77
	9.14	6.12	
General Electric	0.0029	0.0016	0.84
	9.75	0.31	
Goodyear Tire	0.0146	0.0000	0.30
	6.04	-2.24	
IBM	0.0304	0.0173	0.87
	2.02	0.23	

Table 5.5 (continued)
Estimation of investment model under dividend policy II

Model: $\frac{I}{K} = \beta_0 + \beta_1 Q_2 + e_t$ t-statistic below			
Firm	β_0	β_1	R^2
International Paper	0.0115	0.0000	0.79
	17.25	-6.98	
Merck	0.0418	0.0275	0.78
	10.6	5.91	
3M	0.0239	0.0192	0.80
	1.16	5.80	
Proctor and Gamble	0.0353	0.0105	0.83
	6.99	5.90	
Sears	0.0290	0.0145	0.68
	6.40	5.70	
Texaco	0.0140	0.0054	0.80
	9.67	3.02	
Union Carbide	0.0255	0.00000	0.32
	6.57	0.34	
United Technologies	0.0784	-0.0001	0.56
	2.02	-0.23	

Summary of findings

Interpretations of the results from testing the reduced-form investment equation in Chapter 4 weakly support the hypothesis that, the tax-adjusted Q is an important determinant of investment behaviour. Coefficients on Q and lagged Q are small but significant across firm size categories under both dividend policy specifications. It is also important to recognize that, in attempting to measure and draw conclusions about tax effects on firm investment in this model, other factors, such as the cost of funds to the firm and profitability of investment, are held constant in this study. Focusing on Q and investment growth aggregates over time, there appears to be a very weak correspondence, as depicted in Figures 5.2 and 5.3. Figure 5.2 indicates that investment growth was relatively weak during the 1980s. In Figure 5.3 Q_2 values defined under dividend policy II seem to be increasing in the 1980s with a distinct drop following 1986. Under dividend policy I, Q_1 shows little growth over time, indicating a better correspondence than Q_2 to the sluggish investment growth of the 1980s. However, both Qs drop after 1986 indicating a decrease in the firm's marginal incentive to invest, which is consistent with the 1986 tax reform measures, but inconsistent with the slow investment growth of the post-1986 period.

Conclusions

Overall investment rates did not fluctuate outside their normal range in the 1980s indicating an ambiguous effect of the tax reforms on corporate investment growth. The reasons for this weak evidence on the link between taxes and investment are not clear. One reason might be the violation of assumptions of the theoretical model, or simple model misspecification in the empirical estimations. This might include exclusion of important effects, or inability to determine the proper lags to use in measuring the effects of a tax reform effect on firm investment behaviour. In addition, with such frequent tax reforms, one wonders how tax-payer expectations are formed; specifically, whether they really regard any tax code change as a permanent one.

Investment models estimated using q, Q_1,Q_1' and Q_2 generally support the tax-adjusted Q theory of investment for the period 1970-1989 based on statistical significance measures of R^2 and t-values. Conclusions based on signs of the coefficients also provide support of the investment model as a test of correlation between investment and Q.

Comparison of Tobin's q and tax-adjusted Q_2 indicate that some firms fared better in the 1980s than others. This uneven effect across firms provides evidence that only some firms experienced improved incentives to invest, while others appear to have had incentives reduced. In addition, the importance of using a tax-adjusted Q to measure firm investment incentives is underscored by the fact that the values of Tobin's q and the tax-adjusted Qs are different over time.

Notes

1. From Hayashi (1982) we know that all we can measure directly is the firm's average Q, even though Q theory is based on the marginal Q. I therefore use the observable average Q as a proxy for the marginal Q in this work.

2. See Turnovsky (1990), pp. 491-521.

3. Of the original 30 firms in the Summers study, 13 were excluded for reasons which include continuity within the *COMPUSTAT II* data set for the period of this study, merger activities and missing values.

4. Historically, firms with no apparent incentives to invest may still do so. One obvious weakness in this specification is failure of the model's assumption that capital is homogeneous and malleable. That is to say, in the real world, even firms with low market values can and do find some type of investment desirable.

5. Summers also found a first-order serial correlation problem, but chose not to transform the data because most of the power in the relation between investment and q is found at lower frequencies. In this case, transforming the data would place a larger weight on high frequencies and may possibly be inappropriate.

6 Theory and evidence from panel data

Introduction

Fazzari, Hubbard and Peterson (1988) conclude that Q is at best one of the few significant explanatory variables in determining firm investment behaviour. However, this study on US firm behaviour did not explicitly model the firm's dividend process. Devereux and Schiantarelli (1989) point out that, without modelling the dividend process of the firm, it is not possible to determine which firms are constrained by their earnings.

This chapter estimates an investment model which incorporates two alternative processes for explaining firm dividend behaviour. The methodology, which is based on Hayashi and Inoue (1991), takes into account the cross-sectional and time series nature of the *COMPUSTAT II* data in estimations. This approach avoids Q-related econometric problems by using an instrumental variable technique to account for the endogeneity of Q and cash flow, and employing a Generalized Method of Moments (GMM) estimation technique to correct for heteroscedasticity in the data.

This chapter outlines a process for testing the sensitivity of investment to liquidity constraints for a panel of 220 US firms from 1975 to 1988. Using the two definitions of Q developed in Chapter 2, this framework will also allow us to test for robustness of the Q investment model to dividend policy specification.

Econometric issues

Many previous Q studies are plagued with two non-trivial econometric problems. The first econometric problem is that both Q and cash flow are endogenous.

Hayashi and Inoue (1991) verify the endogenous nature of Q by showing how it is essentially a function of technology shocks, and is therefore econometrically endogenous. The error term in the Q model then represents technology shocks to the profit function, which includes adjustment costs. When this endogeneity is not accounted for, it is not surprising that variables such as output and cash flow which are affected by technology shocks, are significant when added to the Q model estimations. Therefore it is important to correct for this problem when attempting to estimate an investment equation which contains Q, cash flow, and output on the right hand side.

The second econometric difficulty stems from the possibility that the variances across firms may not be equal. That is to say that, by using a panel data set rather than data from a random sample, one must correct for the possibility that variances may differ across firms. Further, as Gilchrist (1989) notes, if the investment model is misspecified such that Q is no longer a sufficient statistic for investment, then cash flow may simply be capturing this misspecification. These problems associated with previous Q estimations will be addressed presently.

The issue of misspecification is explored by estimating the Q investment equation with and without cash flow to test for the significance of cash flow in the model. However, I do not discriminate between capital and labour inputs in the model. This simplification is justified by Wildasin (1984) who has shown that, under a specific set of assumptions, including the Hicks aggregation, Q is independent of the composition of investment.[1]

The problem of endogeneity of Q and cash flow is resolved by using a set of lagged endogenous variables as instruments in the estimation. Specifically, if we assume an error term in our investment model (u_{it}) that is linearly additive, consisting of a permanent component (v_i) which contains all of the correlation across firms, and a temporary component (w_{it}) which is serially uncorrelated, then we can remove the permanent component by first differencing the data. This technique effectively controls for possible firm-specific effects in the data.[2]

The correlation of the temporary component of the error term with our right hand side variables can be resolved by using an instrumental variable approach with values of the lagged endogenous variables as valid instruments. To account for the fact that the variances are not likely to be equal across firms, we can use a GMM estimation technique to obtain heteroscedastic consistent parameter estimates. This two-step procedure minimizes an objective function using an optimal weighting matrix, where each equation is weighted by an estimate of the inverse of the standard error of the equation to correct for cross-equation heteroscedasticity.

Generalized Method of Moments Estimation

The Generalized Method of Moments (GMM) Estimation procedure is a non-linear instrumental variable technique that estimates parameters by fitting sample moments to population moments. This method was popularized by Hansen and Singleton (1982) for estimating first-order conditions of dynamic optimization problems.

In matrix notation, we can specify a system of $(t-1)$ equations in a reduced form as:

$$Y_t = \beta Z_t + e_t,$$

where Y_t is a single-dimensional matrix of dependent variables, Z_t is a matrix of endogenous variables, and e_t is the error term of the equation. Since Z_t is endogenous, we need to find valid instruments; here we can use lagged endogenous variables as valid instruments.

The GMM estimator, $\hat{\beta}$, is then given by:

$$\hat{\beta} = \left(Z'XV^{-1}X'Z\right)^{-1}Z'XV^{-1}X'Y$$

where X is a block diagonal matrix of instruments and V^{-1} is the inverse of the weighted sample covariance.

$\hat{\beta}$ minimizes the objective function:

$$J = N\left(\frac{\varepsilon'X}{N}\right)V^{-1}\left(\frac{X'\varepsilon}{N}\right) \sim \chi^2_{(m-n)},$$

where N is the sample size and ε is the stacked error vector. The J-statistic is asymptotically distributed as a χ^2 with $(m-n)$ degrees of freedom, where m is the total number of instruments or orthogonality conditions, and n is the number of parameters. The J-statistic can then be used to test the set of over-identifying restrictions that there are more orthogonality conditions than parameters.

Computation of parameter estimates

Computation of parameter estimates requires a two-step procedure. The algorithm can be outlined as follows:[3]

Step 1

(1) Choose starting values for the parameters.

(2) Calculate β using the initial parameter values.

(3) Compute $V = \sigma_{tv} \left(\frac{X_t' X_v}{N} \right)$.

(4) Set the weight matrix, $W = V^{-1}$.

(5) Use the weight matrix to minimize the J-statistic.

Here σ_{tv} is a consistent estimate of $cov\left(\varepsilon_t' \varepsilon_v \right)$, and the instrumental variable set X_t includes lagged and future endogenous variables that do not overlap with the time periods over which the first difference is taken. Step 1 produces consistent but not asymptotically efficient estimates.

Step 2

(1) Re-compute the weight matrix as outlined above using the final parameter estimates derived in Step 1.

(2) Use this new weight matrix to minimize the J-statistic.

This gives the most efficient estimates among the class of estimators that minimize a function such as J. T times the resulting J-statistic will be distributed χ^2, with degrees of freedom equal to the number of independent orthogonality conditions.

The reduced investment model

In Chapter 4, the Q model is derived from the first-order conditions of the firm's dynamic optimization problem with adjustment costs. Assuming competitive firms with constant returns to scale production technologies, the marginal adjustment cost of investment should be equal to the shadow price of capital after taxes. The resulting Q investment model has the following testable implications. First, is cash flow a significant determinant of investment? And second, how sensitive is the Q model to alternative specifications of Q based on dividend policy assumptions?

The following Q investment equation is estimated for 14 years of annual *COMPUSTAT II* data subdivided by firm size. Hayashi and Inoue (1991) discuss the appropriateness of using a generalized method of moments procedure to estimate the Q equation model using a set of instruments that are orthogonal to the error term under the null hypothesis of no misspecification. The empirical model can be specified:

$$\frac{I_{jt}}{K_{jt}} = b_0 + b_1 \frac{I_{jt-1}}{K_{jt-1}} + b_2 Q_{jt}^i + b_3 Q_{jt-1}^i + b_4 \frac{CF_{jt}}{K_{jt}} + e_{jt}$$

(6.1)

where Q_{jt-1}^i is firm j's Q at the beginning of the period t under dividend policy specification i, and Q_{jt}^i is firm j's Q at the end of period t, under dividend policy specification i. The purpose of including Qs from both periods is to account for the possibility that cash flow may simply provide new information not contained in the beginning of period t's Q. CF_{jt} is firm j's cash flow for period t, and the error term is the forcing variable from the investment adjustment cost function. $\frac{I_{jt-1}}{K_{jt-1}}$ is firm j's investment in period $t - 1$. Chirinko (1987), and others, have established the importance of including lagged investment in the Q model specification.[4]

Since e_{jt} is not correlated with variables dated $t - 1$ or earlier by assumption, Equation 6.1 can be estimated using an instrumental variable approach, with instruments consisting of once and twice-lagged values of $Q, \frac{I}{K}, \frac{Y}{K}, \frac{CF}{K}$ and time dummies to account for time-related anomalies in the data.

Significance of the cash flow variable can be determined by estimating the investment equation with and without cash flow. Under the null hypothesis that the coefficient on cash flow is not statistically different from zero, the difference in the values of the resulting objective functions times the number of observations is distributed χ_Δ^2 with one degree of freedom. The robustness of the Q model to the different dividend policy assumptions I and II can be examined by comparing the results of the specification tests.

Empirical results

Tables 6.1, 6.2, and 6.3 show summary statistics on all the firms across the sample time period as well as by firm size. Firm size is based on the replacement cost of plant, property and equipment of the firm over the sample period. Size 1 denotes firms with capital assets valued at less than \$35 million, Size 2 denotes firms valued at more than \$35 million but less than \$110 million, Size 3 denotes firms valued at greater than \$110 million but less than \$350 million, and Size 4 denotes firms who had capital assets valued in excess of \$350 million. The cut-off values for these groups were selected to divide the entire sample into four groups of roughly equal size.

Investment I, sales Y, and cash flow CF are all normalized by K, the capital stock in each period in order to focus on the growth of the variables of interest. RE measures the firm's level of retained earnings, and the debt/equity ratio is calculated as changes in firms short-term plus long-term debt holdings divided by changes in the firm's equity issues. DIV/OI is the ratio of the firm's dividend payment to the operating income of the firm. Appendix B contains details on the construction of these variables.

In Table 6.1 we find that the largest firm sizes 3, and 4, have Q_1 and Q_2 values above the mean of the sample. This would be consistent with the notion that larger firms faced lower marginal costs of adjustment during the sample period than smaller firms. It should be kept in mind that the terms 'larger' and 'smaller' in this sample do not span the entire possible range of firm sizes in the general population. All the firms in this study are $S\&P$ publicly held firms, not single-owner private businesses, so they can in a sense all be considered 'large' with respect to the total population of firms. It is also clear that cash flow, retained earnings and the debt/equity ratios are much higher for the largest firm size than the smaller three size groups.

Tables 6.2 and 6.3 list means of some of the firms' important variables from 1975 to 1988 for each year. Investment growth and Q values seemed to have generally increased until the early to mid 1980s then dropped off somewhat after 1986.

Tables 6.4 and 6.5 report the results from estimating Equation 6.1 with and without cash flow for the overall sample and four sub-sample groups divided by firm size. Table 6.4 contains the results of tests for over-specification of the model and the significance of cash flow under dividend policy I. The χ^2 statistic for the investment regression, run both with and without cash flow, tests the hypothesis of over- identifying restrictions in the model with $(m - n)$ degrees of freedom, where m is the total number of instruments, or orthogonality conditions, and n is the number of parameters. The χ^2_Δ statistic can then be interpreted as a test of the significance of cash flow in the model with one degree of freedom. Focusing on χ^2_Δ, cash flow is significant for the All Firms category, as well as for the largest firm size group at the 5 percent level. Cash flow is not found to be significant at the 5 percent or 10 percent levels for firm sizes 1, 2 and 3.

Table 6.5 displays the results of tests under dividend policy assumption II. Looking at the All Firms category, the hypothesis of non-significant cash flow is easily rejected at the 5 percent level. Furthermore, when we break down the firms by size, we find that cash flow appears to be significant for the two largest firm categories at the 5 percent level.

While the result that cash flow matters most for larger firms may seem counter-intuitive, these findings are consistent with those of Gilchrist and Devereux and Schiantarelli. This result may simply reflect the fact that larger firms may have a lower *relative* cash flow, or that they have higher agency costs built in due to a more diverse ownership structure.

Comparing the results between dividend policy assumptions I and II, we find that both model specifications show a similar pattern in significance of cash flow variable as one moves from the smaller to the larger firms; consistent with the pattern of cash flow significance found in Devereux and Schiantarelli (1989) for British firms.

These results support the hypothesis that the Q investment model is robust with respect to assumptions about the nature of the dividend payout process.

Table 6.1
Variable means by firm size
1975-1988

	Standard Deviations below				
Variable Means	All firms (obs=3332)	Size 1 (obs=903)	Size 2 (obs=873)	Size 3 (obs=866)	Size 4 (obs=690)
I/K	0.276 0.13	0.272 0.24	0.261 0.11	0.282 0.19	0.268 0.17
Y/K	3.881 6.4	5.163 3.8	3.278 1.8	3.577 2.8	3.498 3.2
CF/K	1.056 2.2	0.793 0.78	0.784 0.62	0.778 0.69	2.076 4.6
RE	0.406 1.1	0.253 1.2	0.265 0.26	0.288 0.21	0.931 1.9
Debt/Equity	0.833 2.6	0.865 2.9	0.648 1.3	0.756 1.4	0.931 4.2
Div/OI	0.023 0.09	0.038 0.06	0.025 0.14	0.013 0.04	0.007 0.02
Q_1	1.16 0.91	1.03 0.83	1.12 0.87	1.28 1.01	1.24 0.87
Q_2	1.77 1.08	1.63 1.01	1.69 0.99	1.89 1.11	1. 90 1.14

Table 6.2
Variable means by year
1975-1981

		Standard Deviations below					
Variable Means	1975	1976	1977	1978	1979	1980	1981
I/K	0.15	0.19	0.20	0.22	0.24	0.27	0.29
	0.11	0.03	0.08	0.05	0.10	0.12	0.13
Y/K	1.445	2.13	2.36	2.71	3.07	3.56	3.96
	1.95	2.1	2.6	3.4	5.5	6.8	7.5
CF/K	0.248	0.472	0.521	0.598	0.713	0.812	0.918
	0.37	0.19	0.42	0.44	1.21	1.41	1.40
RE	0.171	0.223	0.246	0.279	0.334	0.402	0.446
	0.25	0.26	0.33	0.41	0.62	0.9	0.99
Debt/Equity	0.720	0.630	0.650	0.610	0.610	0.600	0.740
	1.70	1.10	1.60	0.80	0.60	0.60	1.50
Div/OI	0.047	0.043	0.034	0.031	0. 029	0.042	0.019
	0.07	0.09	0.05	0.04	0.06	0.24	0.06
Q_1	0.50	0.99	0.95	0.92	1.04	1. 19	1.10
	1.22	0.69	0.63	0.56	0.72	0.93	0.73
Q_2	0.82	1.52	1.52	1.49	1.69	1.76	1.69
	1.3	0.72	0.66	0.61	0.80	1.04	0.87

Table 6.3
Variable means by year
1982-1988

	Standard Deviations below						
Variable Means	1982	1983	1984	1985	1986	1987	1988
I/K	0.31	0.31	0.32	0.32	0.32	0.31	0.31
	0.17	0.18	0.17	0.15	0.16	0.17	0.18
Y/K	4.07	4.27	4.77	4.72	4.76	5.18	5.42
	6.90	8.10	9.30	9.80	8.90	9.90	11.8
CF/K	1.03	1.15	1.37	1.47	1.64	1.83	1.98
	1.70	1.10	2.40	3.00	3.50	3.60	4.10
RE	0.464	0.472	0.478	0.497	0.484	0.491	0.710
	1.10	1.10	1.10	1.10	1.10	1.30	2.70
Debt/Equity	0.69	0.79	0.69	0. 95	1.20	1.30	1.40
	1.20	2.80	1.3	0.09	2.30	4.40	5.60
Div/OI	0.012	0.009	0.007	0.007	0.006	0.005	0.008
	0.01	0.03	0.01	0.01	0.01	0.01	0.04
Q_1	1.33	1.55	1.35	1.53	1. 55	1.17	1.09
	0.88	0.98	0.81	1.05	1.02	0. 86	0.79
Q_2	1.90	2.19	1.98	2.27	2.42	1.82	1.79
	1.02	1.19	0.95	1.17	1.37	1.11	1.01

Table 6.4
IV GMM Estimation of Q_1 investment model
under dividend policy I

Coefficient (Standard Errors)	$\frac{CF_t}{K_t}$	$\frac{I_{t-1}}{K_{t-1}}$	Q_t	Q_{t-1}	χ^2	χ^2_Δ
All Firms	.1503	.1915	.1147	-.1345	13.95	9.23
	(.17)	(.14)	(.60)	(.12)		
	-	.1998	.0032	.0150	4.72	
	-	(.41)	(.44)	(.06)		
Size 1	.3558	.4512	-.0016	-.0268	1.83	0.52
	(.16)	(.10)	(.18)	(.05)		
	-	.7992	.2019	.0283	0.31	
	-	(.18)	(.73)	(.08)		
Size 2	.3227	.6328	-.0227	- .0341	7.44	1.23
	(.73)	(.58)	(.16)	(.05)		
	-	.7295	.2769	-.0165	6.21	
	-	(.18)	(.21)	(.10)		
Size 3	.2591	.4784	-.1731	.0417	2.03	1.89
	(.44)	(.48)	(.07)	(.06)		
	-	.3861	.2440	.8821	0.14	
	-	(.42)	(.49)	(.19)		
Size 4	.7545	.1709	-.0505	.1713	16.9	3.84
	(.48)	(.16)	(.07)	(.04)		
	-	.2205	.9994	.9810	13.11	
	-	(.32)	(.79)	(.69)		

Table 6.5
IV GMM estimation of Q_1 investment model
under dividend policy II

Coefficient (Standard Errors)	$\frac{CF_t}{K_t}$	$\frac{I_{t-1}}{K_{t-1}}$	Q_t	Q_{t-1}	χ^2	χ^2_Δ
All Firms	.1508	.6992	.1138	.0896	32.58	10.79
	(.33)	(.09)	(.06)	(.03)		
	-	.6864	-.0374	.1106	21.79	
	-	(.08)	(.08)	(.03)		
Size 1	2.602	.3993	.0010	.0532	3.38	1.39
	(1.0)	(2.0)	(.68)	(.15)		
	-	4.218	.8371	-.0009	1.99	
	-	(9.2)	(1.7)	(.34)		
Size 2	0.018	1.767	-.7166	-.2077	2.740	1.67
	(.87)	(1.7)	(.65)	(.18)		
	-	3.912	-1.107	-.3489	1.07	
	-	(4.7)	(1.7)	(.48)		
Size 3	.5540	.1636	.0183	-.0599	16.19	12.59
	(.61)	(.57)	(.10)	(.06)		
	-	3.260	-.0684	-.0548	3.60	
	-	(.56)	(.20)	(.12)		
Size 4	.3116	.7273	.2594	.0709	33.50	3.94
	(.49)	(.16)	(.07)	(0.03)		
	-	.8469	.0234	.1068	29.56	
	-	(.12)	(.10)	(.03)		

Conclusions

Results indicate that liquidity constraints are important in the Q investment model. Specifically, when we move from smaller to larger firms, we find that cash flow is a significant determinant of investment in the model. Furthermore, we find that this pattern generally holds under both Q specifications; that is, cash flow is significant whether we define the dividend payout process as one where the firm pays a fixed dividend to stock holders on their equity or, more traditionally, as one that pays the difference between after-tax profits minus the costs of adjustment. Overall, these results imply that the Q theory model is robust to alternative Qs based on dividend-payout behaviour.

In addition, while means of investment growth appear relatively stable over the period of the study, Q values displayed much more variation. Sharp declines in both Qs after 1986 support the notion that the net impact of the 1986 tax reforms on capital investment was an increase in the marginal cost of investment to the firm.

Notes

1. See Wildasin (1984), pp. 203-10.

2. This specification of the error term $u_{it} = v_i + w_{it}$ is supported by findings of Hayashi and Inoue (1991). Further, Bond, Elston, Mairesse and Mulkay (1994) discuss the importance of controlling for firm-specific effects in studies of this nature through first-differencing of the data.

3. For a complete derivation of the GMM estimator see Hansen and Singleton (1982).

4. One interesting variation for future research might be to incorporate a measure of liquidity constraint effects directly into the Q definition.

5. See Chirinko (1987), pp. 69-87.

7 Summary

Conclusions on tax reform impacts

Reality and rhetoric in perspective

Nobody can claim perfect foresight with respect to the impact of tax reform on investment, and certainly the Reagan administration was no exception. On the other hand it should be possible to design policies which are successful in attaining both the correct direction and order of magnitude in terms of their targeted impacts on various economic factors.

In terms of evaluating the overall success of policy makers in the 1980s, we should ask whether the reforms moved the economy closer to the policy targets or further away. Stated in these terms, for whatever reasons, it is now clear that these reforms were by and large unsuccessful in attaining their objectives. In fact, many of the reform policies, in spite of the rhetoric, seem to have made America's economic woes worse.

The tax cuts which were to have stimulated increased work efforts did so to only a very small degree. Further, the weak impact was predictable based on the available studies on work effort response to after-tax wage increases. These labour studies indicated a reasonable response to be a full order of magnitude less than the administration had counted on. In fact, in order for the tax cuts to have increased investment, the US would have had to have grown at a rate which was clearly at variance with historical trends.

For example, just to maintain federal revenues at the pre-tax cuts level, the percentage increase in the work effort induced by the tax cuts would have had to have been 2.5 times as great as the percentage increase in the after-tax wage rate itself. Of course, to increase tax revenues through the tax cut incentives, the percentage increase in work effort would have to be even greater.[1] In other words, the administration's recovery plan was based on incentive effects which were unrealistically high, based on everything we knew at the time.

In terms of the actual impact of this work stimulus on federal revenues, it is estimated that this increase in work effort resulted in perhaps $16 billion additional tax revenues by 1986. Not a bad result in itself, until weighed against the net reduction in tax revenues of nearly $140 billion caused by the reforms, leaving a record deficit of $221 billion in 1986.[2]

In turn, the burgeoning deficit aggravated the low investment problem, because it absorbed much of what little savings there were from the private sector.

Just to finance the new deficit and maintain the same net investment rate without borrowing from abroad would have required a net private savings rate of 12 percent alone. This is nearly 50 percent higher than the postwar savings rate of 8 percent. Of course, to expect savings to finance either a growing deficit or additional capital formation would have required an even larger rate of savings.

The 1981 tax reform Act was in fact designed to address the low national savings problem by allowing individuals to save tax-free in an IRA account up to $2,000 annually, to establish tax-free Keogh accounts, and pay a lower tax on capital gains income. However, in spite of these efforts, the predicted rise in private savings never materialized. Many individuals shifted their targeted savings amount from a simple savings account to one of the newer tax-free forms of savings, but the total amount saved did not change. In other words, the predicted rate at which people saved did not increase. The Reagan administration's reasons for believing that the rate of savings would increase were not contradictory to economic theory, but can be characterized as a very optimistic prediction of people's response to the reforms.

In addition, according to the new plan, firms were to have increased their investment because they had new tax breaks which gave them a higher after-tax income than they had before. The additional revenue was to have increased the cash flow of the firms and made more funds available internally to finance investment in capital. All of which is economically sound, except for two things. First, the firms were free to use the increased funds for any purpose, not just investment; and second, many of the 1986 tax reforms actually decreased the firm's incentive to invest in capital stock. Empirical results support the hypothesis that, while the firm's investment function is sensitive to cash flow, firms were probably slow to invest because, in many cases, the reforms caused the marginal cost of capital to increase, reducing incentives for the firm to invest.

Firm level evidence

Examining a cross-section of 17 large US stock-issuing firms over the 1980s we find that the tax reforms affected firms differently. Whether intended or not, the

88

reforms had uneven effects on profitability of firms, some being left with higher marginal costs of investment and others with a lower marginal cost of investment after the reforms. At an industry level, this uneven effect persisted as some industries, particularly the capital intensive and technologically oriented industries, were hurt more than others. This effect was particularly strong following the 1986 TRA. The net impact of this particular tax reform actually led to an increase in the marginal cost of investment across all industries, in spite of the reduction in the statutory tax rate.

A time series analysis of firms in the study over the sample period indicates that the marginal incentive for the firm to invest, as measured by Q, was not outside its historical range in the 1980s, but did show a particular decline after 1986. Undertaking these studies also underlines the importance of firm- level studies, rather than relying solely on evidence aggregated at the national level which provide, only a sort of 'averaged' response to the reforms. Further, from a national policy perspective it is critical to know if a particular industry is adversely affected or perhaps subsidized in terms of national strategy in promoting international competitiveness. It is also important to know if the results we see at the national level stem from only a small group of firms doing very well, with most worse off, or a majority of firms doing somewhat better.

Results of comparing the gap between the tax-adjusted Q and non-tax- adjusted Q indicate that the gap has decreased between 1978 and 1988. That is to say that the tax adjustment to the firm's marginal cost of investment decreased from the 1970s to the 1980s on average. This is not to support the notion, as some have argued, that the reforms are ineffectual in affecting firm investment behaviour. Rather, I interpret this as evidence that the more recent revisions in the tax code have included a sort of mixed bag of tax-based incentive effects, some of which tended to cancel each other out in terms of providing a clear signal to firms on investment. In fact, any future tax reform will have to consider more carefully the precise mix of incentives provided. A cohesive package of investment incentives for the firm should focus on the *net* impact to the firm of all the reforms, rather than focusing on single provision as if it was introduced in a vacuum without conflicting effects of other reform measures.

Analyzing the data as panel of firm behaviour over time, indicates that liquidity constraints, as measured by cash flow, are indeed an important determinant of investment. This result was strengthened by the fact that cash flow was significant even when controlling for dividend payout behaviour of the firm. This indicates that it might be advantageous for future policy makers to consider the impacts of tax reform to the firm's liquidity constraint when considering investment incentives. Policy makers could effectively argue that measures to loosen the liquidity constraint may also increase capital formation.

In spite of the formidable challenge for policy makers in the 1990s, we gain by analyzing the difficulties of the previous efforts. These lessons of the 1980s about what did and did not work are useful when considering directions for tax reform in the 1990s. What is also important is to consider new tax alternatives or policy measures to address the problems of increasing savings, investment, and overall productivity without worsening the federal deficit. One source of alternative ideas could be examples provided by other countries who are more successful in balancing their revenue needs with investment incentives.

Directions for future tax reform

One lesson we learned from the 1980s is that, while two taxes may generate the same revenue for the government, some taxes provide more incentives for the firm to invest in capital than others. Dollar for dollar, a cut in the statutory corporate tax rate is less likely to end up as a dollar spent on equipment than a dollar equivalent provided through an investment tax credit. Reinstating the ITC and ACRS would go a long way toward providing the pre-1986 investment incentives to the firm. Even if coupled with revenue neutral corporate tax increases, this would effectively reduce the cost of capital to the firm and increase capital formation.

Raising the national savings rate back up to even its former 1980 level would also do much to improve both economic growth and international competitiveness. Since one of the key problems is the size of the federal budget deficit, reducing this should be the focus of future reforms, rather than fiddling unsuccessfully, as before, with private savings plans incentives. Reducing the deficit can be done in a number of ways, but some important alternatives are consumption-based taxes and real federal spending reductions.

The consumption tax alternative

One way to reduce the deficit is to introduce a new source of tax revenue. In selecting an optimal tax there are also several important considerations, one of which is the fairness of the tax or the distributional effects. This consideration would include such decisions as how the tax burden is distributed. For example, some people feel it is fair if persons in equal positions are treated equally, while others feel a fair tax is one that redistributes resources in a socially desirable manner. A second goal of a good tax is to minimize the excess burden, which we can define as the difference between the taxes paid by the individual or firm and the revenues collected by the government. This is sometimes referred to as the ' efficiency' of the tax.

Other considerations might include compliance and enforcement issues of the tax, as well as its political impact. This means that a tax is feasible only if it can be collected and enforced in some reasonable fashion. And, of course, in reality, we know that if a tax is going to jeopardize the re-election of a government official, it is unlikely to be instituted, regardless of its merits in terms of efficiency or fairness.

Value Added Taxes, or VAT, are one attractive candidate for increasing tax revenues without increasing the marginal income tax rates. This consumption tax, which is similar to the US's existing retail sales tax, is a popular form of tax revenue in Latin America and Europe.[3] Jorgenson (1993) points out that the US currently relies too heavily on income taxes relative to either sales or property taxes. The advantages of VAT are well documented.

VAT do not distort the household's intertemporal consumption choices, nor do they affect the investment decision of the firm if the time paths of the market rate of interest and the employment of labour are given.[4] This means that it does not negatively affect the growth path of the economy. In other words, VAT do not distort choices or reduce incentives to save or invest. This neutrality of VAT make it a good candidate among the various possible tax instruments available to increase potential tax revenues.

Like the retail tax, VAT are a relatively easy tax both to implement and reinforce. Critics argue that this tax unfairly burdens the poor, since the poor consume, and therefore contribute, a higher percentage of their incomes. However, this tax can be designed to be as progressive as desired, with exemptions for necessities and higher rates on other non-essential goods. Summers (1987) points out that this sort of tax could be expected to significantly increase national savings and therefore help the national growth problem.

Capital financing and corporate ownership

Since it has been established that liquidity constraints affect investment behaviour, any reform which targets investment incentives should consider the availability of investment funds to the firm as well. There is international evidence which suggests that the relationships between firms and creditors may be important in the firm's real and financial decisions.

Hoshi, Kashyap and Scharfstein (1991) found that Japanese manufacturing firms which had close ties to banks had investment functions that were less liquidity-constrained than firms that did not have the ties. In this context, ties describe a situation where the firm is a member of an industrial organizational group or *Keiretsu*.

In Germany, banks sometimes hold equity in firms, sit on supervisory boards, as well as provide external financing to the firm. In fact, 27 of the largest 150 stock-issuing German manufacturing *Aktiengesellschaft* AG firms had bank ownership ranging from 10 to 70 percent of outstanding stock of the firm in 1991. These firms, for whatever reasons, comprise some of the largest and most successful firms in Germany.[5] Elston (1993b) and Elston and Albach (1995) find evidence that bank-owned and bank-affiliated firms in Germany exhibit investment functions which are less sensitive to liquidity constraints than independent firms. In addition, studies on France, Germany and the UK indicate that this relationship may also reduce the number of hostile take-overs, buy-ins and buy-outs.[6] In fact, several studies have provided evidence which supports the notion that the information sharing which occurs in such relationships results not only in an investment function which is less liquidity constrained, but possibly a more efficient allocation of capital within the firm.[7][8]

Theoretical economists have frequently argued that close bank-firm relationships provide incentives and induce monitoring which is beneficial to the long-run health of the firm, the stockholders and thus society as a whole. In the event that the owner and primary external creditor of the firm is a bank, the flow of information shared is expected to be greater than the case where the bank acts only as a creditor to the firm. If this flow of information reduces informational asymmetries, then one would expect a reduction in the risk associated with providing investment funds, and thus, a reduction in the costs associated with financing a particular project.

Unfortunately, empirical work is lagging behind theoretical developments in this area of financial economics, and it is clear that more studies must be conducted before any definitive conclusions can be drawn about causality in these complicated relationships. In this regard, however, it would be reasonable for reform analysts to further investigate the importance of ownership structure and capital financing on firm behaviour, with an eye to a better alignment of the goals of managers, owners and society.[9]

Each of these suggestions offer alternative directions to consider in evaluating the firm's ability to invest, without causing a reduction in savings incentives or tax revenues needed to improve the government budget deficit. But they are only suggestions out of a multitude of choices. Choices which will define America in the 1990s and beyond.

Notes

1. See Friedman (1988), p. 242.

2. Ibid.

3. For a detailed description of the differences and similarities of the VAT and the retail sales tax see Musgrave and Musgrave (1973).

4. See Sinn (1987).

5. See Elston (1993) .

6. See Franks and Mayers (1990), pp. 189-232.

7. See Hoshi, Kashyap and Scharfstein (1991), pp. 33-60.

8. See Porter (1992), pp. 65-82.

9. This process should involve evaluating the current financial markets structure in the US, including the Glass-Steagall Act of 1934, which prohibits banks from taking equity positions in firms.

Appendix A

Derivation of Summers' Q_2

The Q theory of investment model

Based on Summers (1981), we can model the behaviour of the firm in accordance with the traditional neoclassical production function (F) with the firm using inputs of capital, (K), and labour, (L). In this model I assume that both marginal products are positive but diminishing such that $F_l > 0$, $F_k > 0$ and $F_{ll} < 0$, $F_{kk} < 0$ and $F_{kk}F_{ll} - F_{kl}^2 = 0$, where single and double subscripts denote first and second derivatives of the production function with respect to factor inputs. We can also assume non-monopoly rents, a constant returns to scale production function with homogeneity of factors, and complementarity of factor inputs such that $F_{kl} = F_{lk} > 0$.

The gross profits of the firm can then be defined as

$$R = pF\,(K, L) - wL - prbk, \qquad (A.1)$$

where p is the current price level and F is the production function of the firm based on capital (K) and labour (L) inputs. The term w is the real wage rate, which is determined by the market because the firm is a price taker in this model. The term r is the nominal rate of interest, b is the fixed share of the capital stock that the firm maintains as debt, and the term $pbkr$ reflects the fact that the firm expenses interest payments on the debt.

If corporate profits are taxed at τ_f and the remainder is either paid out as dividends (D) or kept as retained earnings (RE), then the following equation describes corporate sources and uses of funds

$$(1 - \tau_f)\,R = D + RE. \qquad (A.2)$$

Since equipment requires installation, we define a convex cost of adjustment, H, as a function of investment, I, and capital, K, by

$$H\left(\frac{I}{K}\right). \tag{A.3}$$

Costs of adjustment enter the model because firms cannot costlessly and instantly adjust the capital stock, rather they face costs of equipment installation and removal. Here we define a marginal cost of adjustment as an increasing function of the rate of investment where H_I, $H_{II} > 0$. This means that, as the firm increases investment, it becomes more costly to do so, that is to say there exist some diseconomies of scale with respect to increases in capital investment.

The financing constraint facing firms can then be defined:

$$RE + s\dot{E} = (1 - pb)H\left(\frac{I}{K}\right), \tag{A.4}$$

where b is again the fraction of the capital stock maintained as debt, representing bond financing, s is the price of an issue, $\dot{E}$ is the outstanding stock of the firm, and τ_f is the corporate tax rate. The dot notation above the E denotes the time derivative of equity. This equation describes both the sources and uses of funds. In the most general case, financing can come from any combination of these three sources. Throughout the rest of this model, Summers assumes that the firm neither issues new equity nor repurchases existing shares. And, since we allow for bond financing, then $b > 0$.

The value of outstanding equities, V, can then be described as

$$V = sE. \tag{A.5}$$

Hence prices are proportional to the outstanding value of the firm's equity, and from Equations A.2 and 2.4 we then derive an expression for dividends

$$D = (1 - \tau_f)\left[R - C\left(\frac{I}{K}\right)K\right] + s\dot{E}, \tag{A.6}$$

96

where $C\left(\frac{I}{K}\right) = H\left(\frac{I}{K}\right)(1 - pb)$ for notational simplicity. Noting that the cost of capital is defined as the real rate of return on equity, or θ, we can combine Equation A.6 with the consumer optimality condition for equity and the time derivative of Equation A.5 derive the following equation for explaining the evolution of the value of the firm over time:

$$\dot{V} = \frac{\theta}{(1 - \tau_c)}V - \left[(1 - \tau_f)R - C\left(\frac{I}{K}\right)K\right] + \frac{(\tau_y - \tau_c)}{(1 - \tau_c)}D, \qquad (A.7)$$

where θ is the real required rate of return on equities, which is adjusted by 1 minus τ_c, the tax rate on capital gains, and τ_y is the tax rate on ordinary or personal income.

From Equation A.7 we see that, if $\tau_y = \tau_c$, then dividend policy is important to the firm. Applying this dividend rule to Equation A.7 we derive the dividend policy-specific differential equation:

$$\dot{V}_2 = \left(\frac{\theta}{1 - \tau_c}\right)V - \left(\frac{1 - \tau_y}{1 - \tau_c}\right)(1 - \tau_f)\left[R - C\left(\frac{I}{K}\right)K\right]e^{-\int_t^s \theta^* du}ds. \qquad (A.8)$$

There are several interesting implications that Equation A.8 suggests. First of all, $\dot{V}_2$ implies that the cost of capital, θ^*, is equal to $\left(\frac{\theta}{1 - \tau_c}\right)$. Focusing on tax policy implications, if all financing comes from RE, then the personal tax rate, τ_y, has no effect on the long-run capital to labour ratio. If, however, all profits of the firm are paid out as dividends, then τ_c, the capital gains tax rate, becomes irrelevant. This rule leads to a long-run undervaluation of equities.

The firm's objective is to maximize the initial value of equity, $V(0)$, with respect to the inputs K, L, I. We can rewrite Equation A.8 in the more generalized form as:

$$\dot{V} = \theta^* V - \gamma(K, L, I). \qquad (A.9)$$

Integrating Equation A.9 we can express the firm's maximization as a function of the dividend policy problem over time as:

$$\text{Max}_{K,L,I} V(0) = \int_t^\infty (1 - \tau_f)\left[R - C\left(\frac{I}{K}\right)K\right]\left(\frac{1 - \tau_d}{1 - \tau_c}\right)e^{-\int_t^s \theta^* du}ds \qquad (A.10)$$

97

s.t.

$$\dot{K}(s) = I(s) - \delta K(s) \qquad (A.11)$$
$$K(0) = K_0. \qquad (A.12)$$

Equation A.10 suggests that the firm wishes to maximize the net present value of net revenues by choosing optimal capital, labour and investment levels subject to capital constraints. The first constraint, $\dot{K}(s)$ describes the capital accumulation path whereby the firm invests to replace a deteriorating proportional constant, δ, of the capital stock K. $K(0)$ is simply the initial capital stock level. At each point in time t then, the firm picks L_t and K_t to maximize the value of the firm, V_t, while the optimal value of investment, I_t, is determined residually from the capital accumulation identity.

If we assume expectations about future dividend payments of the firm are formed with perfect foresight, we can impose the following transversality condition to guarantee a unique solution to our maximization problem:

$$\lim_{s \to \infty} V(s) e^{-\int_t^s \theta^* du} = 0.$$

Rewriting Equation A.10 in terms of observable parameters, the value of the firm can be expressed:

$$V_{2t} = \int_t^\infty \left[\left(F(K_t, L_t) - wL - bK_t r \right) (1 - \tau_f) - \right.$$

$$\left(1 - ITC_t - Z_t - b + (1 - \tau_f) C \left(\frac{I_t}{K_t} \right) \right) I_t + pbK_t \left(\pi - \delta^R \right) \left] \left(\frac{1 - \tau_d}{1 - \tau_c} \right) * \right.$$

$$e^{-\int_t^s \theta^* du} ds + B_t,$$

$$(A.13)$$

where K_t and L_t are factor inputs, wL_t is the labour expense, and rbK_t is the expensed interest on the debt, all of which is adjusted by the statutory corporate tax rate, τ_f. The next part of the expression represents the investment expenses,

98

where ITC_t is the investment tax credit, Z_t is the present value of depreciation allowances, b is the fraction of the capital that the firm maintains as debt, and $(1 - \tau_f) C \left(\frac{I_t}{K_t} \right)$ is the net convex costs of adjustment, all of which is multiplied by investment I_t. All of this is then discounted by $\left(\frac{1-\tau_d}{1-\tau_c} \right)$ times θ^*, the real required rate of return on capital. B_t is the present value of depreciation allowances on existing capital stock. Of course, in maximizing Equation A.13 B_t becomes irrelevant to the firm because it is independent of any current or future decisions.

Tax parameters in Equation A.13 are allowed to change over time, and can be defined as:

$$B(t) = \int_t^\infty \tau_f \delta^T e^{-\delta^T (s-t)} \mu(s) K_t ds \tag{A.14}$$

$$Z(t) = \int_t^\infty \tau_f \delta^T e^{-\delta^T (u-s)} \frac{\mu(u)}{\mu(s)} \left(\frac{1 - \tau_c}{1 - \tau_d} \right) du \tag{A.15}$$

$$\mu(s) = e^{-\int_0^s \theta^* du.} \tag{A.16}$$

Here, $B(t)$ is the present value of depreciation allowances on existing capital stock, which is a function of the corporate tax rate, τ_f, times the statutory depreciation rate on capital, δ^T, discounted by the tax-adjusted required rate of return on capital, θ^*, times the capital stock, K_t. $Z(t)$, the present value of depreciation allowances on new investment, is a function of the corporate tax rate, τ_f, times the statutory depreciation rate on capital, δ^T, discounted by the tax-adjusted required rate of return on capital. The term $\mu(s)$, defines the discount factor which is derived from the consumer optimality conditions for equity. As defined in Equation A.16, it is a function of the required rate of return on capital after corporate, but before personal income taxes and capital gains taxes.

Equation A.13 can be interpreted as the market value of the firm's equity at time t which is equal to the after-tax profits of the firm, minus investment expenses, adjusted for tax and depreciation allowances. Maximizing this equation subject to the capital constraints allows us to derive the following optimality conditions for the firm:

$$F_L = \frac{w}{p} \tag{A.17}$$

99

$$(1 - ITC_t - Z_t - b) + (1 - \tau_f)\left[C\left(\frac{I_t}{K_t}\right) + C'\left(\frac{I_t}{K_t}\right)\frac{I_t}{K_t}\right] = \frac{\lambda_t}{p_t}\left(\frac{1 - \tau_c}{1 - \tau_d}\right) \tag{A.18}$$

$$\left[(1 - \tau_f)(F_k - br) - \left(\frac{I_t}{K_t}\right)^2 C'\left(\frac{I_t}{K_t}\right)(1 - \tau_f) + br\left(\pi - \delta^R\right)\right] =$$
$$\left[-\frac{\dot{\lambda}_t}{p_t} + \frac{\lambda_t}{p_t}(\theta_t^\star)\right]\left(\frac{1 - \tau_c}{1 - \tau_d}\right). \tag{A.19}$$

Equation A.17 suggests that the firm will hire labour until the marginal product of labour is equal to wages, adjusted by the current price level. Equation A.18 characterizes the investment function; it defines a function which links investment to the real shadow price of capital, $\frac{\lambda_t}{p_t}$, the tax parameters and the convex costs of adjustment. Intuitively, the right hand side can be interpreted as the shadow price of an additional unit of capital goods, which should be equal to their marginal cost in after-tax profits on the left hand side of the equation.

The condition for zero investment suggests that Equation A.19 becomes:

$$\frac{\lambda_t}{p_t} = \left(\frac{1 - \tau_d}{1 - \tau_c}\right)[1 - ITC_t - Z_t - b]. \tag{A.20}$$

Equation A.19 describes the evolution of the shadow price of capital. It guarantees that the shadow price of capital equals the present value of future marginal products of a unit of capital.

Derivation of the empirical Q

Because we have a constant returns to scale production technology and homogeneity of the adjustment cost function by definition, then we can derive our empirical Q as follows. From Hayashi (1982) we know:

$$V_t^* - B_t = \gamma p_t K_t, \tag{A.21}$$

where V_t is the stock market value of the firm when the optimal path is followed, B_t is the value of depreciation allowances, which is equal to a fixed proportion, γK_t, of the initial capital stock. The maximum principle implies then that:

$$\lambda_t = \frac{dV_t^*}{dK_t},\tag{A.22}$$

where $\frac{\lambda_t}{p_t}$ is the shadow price of new investment or marginal Q.

Combining Equations A.21 and A.22 we get:

$$\lambda_t = \frac{V_t^* - B_t}{p_t K_t}.\tag{A.23}$$

Combining Equations A.18, A.20, and A.23 we can derive the tax-adjusted Q_2 in terms of observable parameters as:

$$Q_2 = h \left[\frac{\left(\frac{V_t - B_t}{p_t K_t}\right)\left(\frac{1-\tau_d}{1-\tau_c}\right) - 1 + b + ITC_t + Z_t.}{1 - \tau_f} \right]\tag{A.24}$$

Appendix B

Variable construction

All variables used in estimations, except tax, interest rates and prices, were constructed from annual data provided in the *COMPUSTAT II* data set. Estimations were performed on a sub-sample consisting of 220 firms from 1975-1988.

Firm variables

V_t represents the market value of the firm, which is calculated as the market value of debt plus equity. The market value of equity at time t, was determined by adding the end-of-year closing prices on stocks times the number of outstanding shares (E) to the market value of preferred stock and debt. The market value of preferred stock was derived by dividing preferred dividends (PS) by the preferred stock yield (PSY). The market value of debt was proxied by adding the book value of long-term debt to the book value of short-term debt, assuming a real fixed rate of return on equity of 6 percent:

$$V_t = sE + \frac{PS}{PSY} + Debt.$$

Capital stock, K_t, is evaluated at replacement cost based on taxable net property, plant, and equipment:

$$K_t = TNPPE_t = \left(\frac{TNPPE_{t-1} + PPI_t}{PPI_{t-1} + I_t} \right) \times \left(1 - \frac{2}{L} \right),$$

where I_t is investment in period t, PPI_t is the producer price index in period t, $TNPPE_t$ is the taxable net property, plant, and equipment in period t, and L is the useful life of capital goods. The useful life of capital goods is defined as gross property, plant and equipment lagged one period plus current investment, divided by current book value depreciation.

Inventories were also valued at replacement cost. This involved adjusting inventories for both inflation and the inventory method used. Unless inventories were reported as being LIFO, a FIFO equivalent accounting measure was assumed in order to simplify the valuation process. The process for weighting the portion of inventories reported by each method is explained in Summers (1981). Inventories were added to capital stock in the denominator of the tax-adjusted Q.

The present value of future depreciation deductions on investment at time t was calculated as:

$$Z_t = \frac{\tau_d}{\delta + \frac{\rho + \pi}{1 - \tau_c}},$$

where τ_d is the dividend tax rate, δ is the depreciation rate of capital, $(\rho + \pi)$ is the real rate of return expected by investors on equity, adjusted for the capital gains tax rate, τ_c.

B_t is the present value of depreciation allowances on existing capital. This was calculated as :

$$B_t = \frac{\tau_d}{\delta + \frac{\rho + \pi}{1 - \tau_c}} \left(\frac{1 - \tau_d}{1 - \tau_c} \right) P_t K_t,$$

where τ_d is the dividend tax rate, τ_c is the capital gains tax rate, P_t is the price level, and K_t is capital stock.

Tax variables

The reported investment tax credit for each firm represents the accumulated tax deferrals of investment tax credits generated by new capital investments. All tax rates from 1970 to 1978 were taken directly from Summers (1981). Tax rates from 1979 to 1989 were derived as follows: the corporate tax rate, τ_f, which represents the statutory tax rate on corporate income, is derived from Henderson (1986). The tax rates on dividends, τ_d, is the average marginal tax rate on dividend income estimated by Gary Biddle, University of Washington School of Business Administration. The capital gains tax, τ_c, is the average marginal tax rate on capital gains income taken from Henderson (1986).

104

Appendix C

Tobin's q and Q_2 for 17 firms

Table C.1
Tobin's q and tax-adjusted Q_2
for 17 S&P firms
1978 and 1988

Study Year Firm	Summers 1978 q	Q_2	Elston 1988 q	Q_2
ACA	0.658	0.296	1.164	0.8521
American Brands	0.989	1.543	1.956	2.678
American T and T	0.765	0.4852	1.301	1.001
Bethlehem Steel	0.303	-0.807	1.227	1.029
Eastman Kodak	1.607	3.906	1.089	0.667
Exxon	0.744	0.674	1.644	2.003
General Electric	1.444	3.501	1.355	1.065
Goodyear Tire	0.554	-0.181	2.774	5.158
IBM	3.083	9.85	1.30	1.321
International Paper	0.854	0.992	1.716	1.770
Merck	3.026	8.83	1.298	1.052
3M	2.129	5.85	4.058	5.360
Proctor and Gamble	1.703	4.63	1.956	2.014
Sears	2.01	4.26	1.730	1.844
Texaco	0.67	0.177	1.254	0.978
Union Carbide	0.534	0.036	1.277	1.163
United Technologies	1.17	2.198	1.260	1.090

Bibliography

Aoki, M. (1984), 'Shareholders' non-unanimity on investment financing: banks versus individual invests' in Aoki, M. (ed.) *The Economic Analysis of the Japanese Firm*, North-Holland, Amsterdam.

Arellano, M. and Bond, S.R. (1988), 'Dynamic panel data estimation using DPD: a guide for users', *IFS Working Paper*, No. 88/15.

Auerbach, A. (1979), 'Wealth maximization and the cost of capital', *The Quarterly Journal of Economics*, vol. 93, pp. 433-46.

Auerbach, A. and Hassett, K. (1979), 'Investment, tax policy, and the tax reform of 1986', technical report, University of Michigan.

Bernanke, B. (1983), 'The Determinants of Investment: Another look', *The American Economic Review*, vol. 73, no. 2, pp. 71-5.

Bhattacharya, S. (1979), ' Imperfect information, dividend policy and the bird in the hand fallacy', *Bell Journal of Economics*, vol. 10, pp. 259-70.

Bishoff, C. (1971), 'Business investment in the 1970s: A comparison of models', *Brookings Papers on Economic Activity*, no. 1, pp. 13-58.

Blundell, R. Bond, S.,Devereux, M., and Schiantarelli, F. (1992), 'Investment and Tobin's q. Evidence from company panel data, *Journal of Econometrics*, vol. 51, pp. 233-57.

Bond, S. and Meghir, C. (1994), 'Dynamic investment models and the firm's financial policy', *Review of Economic Studies*, no. 61.

Bond, S., Elston, J., Mairesse, J., and Mulkay, B. (1995) 'A comparison of empirical investment equations using company panel data for France, Germany, Belgium, and the UK', forthcoming *Wissenschaftszentrum Berlin* and *Center for Economic Polcy Research* discussion papers.

Brainard, W. and Tobin, J. (1968), 'Pitfalls in financial model building', *The American Economic Review*, vol. 58, no. 2, pp. 99-122.

Brock, W. and Turnovsky, S. (1981), 'The analysis of macroeconomic policies in perfect foresight equilibrium' *The International Economic Review*, No. 22, pp. 179-209.

Chappel, H. and Cheng, D. (1982), 'Expectations Tobin's q and investment: a note', *Journal of Finance*, vol. 37, no. 1, pp. 231-36.

Chirinko, R. (1987), 'Tobin's q and financial policy', *The Journal of Monetary*

Economics, vol. 19, no. 1, pp. 69-87.

Chirinko, R. (1987), 'The ineffectiveness of effective tax rates on business investment: a critique of Feldstein's Fisher-Schultz lecture', *Journal of Public Economics*, vol. 32, no. 3, pp. 369-87.

Chirinko, R. (1988), 'Business tax policy, the Lucas critique, and lessons from the 1980s', *The American Economic Review*, vol. 78, no. 2, pp. 206-10.

Chirinko, R. (1993), 'Business fixed investment spending: A critical survey of modeling strategies, empirical results, and policy implications', *Journal of Economic Literature*, no. 31.

Chirinko, R. (1993), 'Investment, Tobin's q and multiple capital inputs', *Journal of Economic Dynamics and Control*, vol. 17, no. 5-6, pp. 907-28.

Devereux, M. and Schiantarelli, F.(1989), 'Investment, financial factors and cashflow, evidence from UK panel data' in R. Hubbard (ed.) *Asymmetric Information, Corporate Finance, and Investment*, University of Chicago Press, Chicago.

Downs, T. (1990), 'Q and the tax bias theory: The role of depreciation tax shields', mimeograph, University of Alabama.

Elston, J. (1992), 'Tax reform and corporate investment: Theory and evidence of a Q theoretic approach', doctoral dissertation, University of Washington.

Elston, J. (1993a), 'Are Capital Markets Perfect? Evidence from U.S. Panel Data', *Wissenschaftszentrum Berlin Discussion Paper*, No. 93-7.

Elston, J. (1993b), 'Firm Ownership Structure and Investment: Theory and Evidence from German Panel Data', *Wissenschaftszentrum Berlin Discussion Paper*, No. 93-28.

Elston, J. and Albach, H. (1995), 'Bank affiliations and firm capital investment in Germany', *IFO Studien: Zeitschrift fur empirische Wirtschaftsforschung*, Heft 1/95.

Elston, J. (1995), 'Banks, finance and investment in Germany: A review article', forthcoming *Small Business Economics*.

Fazzari, S.M., Hubbard, R.G. and Petersen, B.C. (1988), 'Financing constraints and corporate investment', *Brookings Papers on Economic Activity*, no. 1, pp. 141-95.

Feldstein, M. (1970), 'Corporate taxation and dividend behavior', *The Review of Economic Studies*, vol. 37, pp. 57-72.

Franks, J. and Mayers, C. (1990), 'Capital markets and corporate control: A study of France, Germany, and the UK', *Economic Policy*, vol. 10.

Friedman, B. (1988), *Day of Reckoning*, Random House, New York.

Gertler, M. (1988), 'Financial structure and aggregate economic activity: an overview', *The Journal of Money, Credit and Banking*, vol. 20, no. 3, pp. 559-88.

Gilchrist, S. (1989), 'An empirical analysis of corporate investment and financing hierarchies using firm level panel data', mimeograph, Board of Governors of the Federal Reserve System.

Gordon, R. (1987), *Macroeconomics*, Little, Brown and Company, Toronto.

Hansen, L.P. and Singleton, K.J. (1982), 'Generalized Instrumental Variable Estimation of Nonlinear Rational Expectation Models', *Econometrica*.

Hayashi, F. (1982), 'Tobin's marginal q and average q: A neoclassical interpretation', *Econometrica*, vol. 50, no. 1, pp. 215-24.

Hayashi, F. and Inoue, T. (1991), 'The relation between firm growth and q with multiple capital goods: theory and evidence from panel data on Japanese firms', *Econometrica*, vol. 59, no. 3, pp. 731-53.

Henderson, Y. (1986), 'Lessons from federal reform of business taxes', *New England Economic Review*.

Hoshi, T., Kashyap, A. and Scharfstein, D. (1991), 'Corporate structure, liquidity and investment: evidence from Japanese industrial groups', *Quarterly Journal of Economics*, No. 106.

Hsiao, C. (1990), *Analysis of Panel Data*, Cambridge University Press, Cambridge.

Jorgenson, D. (1993), 'Constructing an Agenda for U.S. Tax Reform', mimeo, AEA meetings, Anaheim, California.

Lintner, J. (1956), 'Distribution of incomes of corporations among dividends, retained earnings, and taxes', *American Economic Review Papers and Procedures*, vol. 5.

Lucas, R. (1976), 'Econometric Policy Evaluation: A Critique', in K. Brunner and H. Meltzer (eds.) *Phillips Curve and the Labour Market*, North-Holland, Amsterdam.

Malkiel, B., Von Furstenberg, M. and Watson, H.S. (1980), *Capital Efficiency and growth: The distribution of investment between industries*, Ballinger, Cambridge, Massachusetts.

Mayer, C. (1986), 'Corporation tax finance and the cost of capital', *Review of Economic Studies*, vol. 53, pp. 93-112.

Mayer, C. (1988), 'New issues in corporate finance', *European Economic Review*.

Meyers, S. (1988),'Tax cuts: Reality or illusion?', technical report, Federal Reserve Bank of Philadelphia.

Miller, M. (1977), 'Debt and taxes',*Journal of Finance*.

Miller, M. and Scholes. M. (1982), 'Dividends and taxes: Some empirical evidence', *Journal of Political Economy*.

Modigliani, F. and Miller, M. (1958), 'The cost of capital, corporate finance and the theory of investment', *The American Economic Review*, vol. 48, no. 3, pp. 261-97.

Modigliani, F. and Miller, M. (1963), 'Corporate income taxes and the cost of capital: a correction', *The American Economic Review*, vol. 53, no. 5, pp. 433-43.

Musgrave, J. and Musgrave M. (1973), *Public Finance in Theory and Practice*, McGraw-Hill, New York.

Myers, S. and Majluf, N. (1984), 'Corporate financing and investment decisions when firms have information that investors do not have', *Journal of Financial Economics*, vol. 13, pp. 187-221.

Nickell, S.J. (1978), *The Investment Decisions of Firms*, Cambridge University Press, Cambridge.

Nelson, R. and Wright, G. (1993), 'The rise and fall of American technological leadership in the postwar period', *Journal of Economic Literature*, vol. 30, no. 4, pp. 1931-64.

Oliner, S. and Rudebush, G. (1989), 'Internal finance and investment: Testing the role of symmetric information and agency costs', *Economic Activity Working Paper*, No. 101.

Porter, M. (1992), 'Capital Disadvantage: America's Failing Capital Investment System', *Harvard Business Review*, September-October.

Poterba, J. and Summers, L. (1983) 'Dividend taxes, corporate investment, and Q', *Journal of Public Finance*, vol. 22, no. 2, pp. 135-67.

Pozdena, R. (1989), 'Tax policy and corporate capital structure', technical report, Federal Reserve Bank of San Francisco.

Salinger, M. and Summers L.H. (1983), *Behaviour simulation methods in tax policy*, Feldstein, M. (ed.), University of Chicago Press, Chicago, pp. 247-87.

Sinn, Hans-Werner (1987), *Capital Income Taxation and Resource Allocation*, Elsevier Science Publishers, New York.

Summers, L.H. (1981), 'Taxation and corporate investment: A q-theory approach', *Brookings Papers on Economic Activity*, no. 1, pp 67-127.

Summers, L.H. (1987), 'A Fair Tax Act That's Bad for Business', *Harvard Business Review*, March-April.

Sumner, M. (1989), 'Investment, Q, and taxes', *Journal of Public Finance*, vol. 44, pp. 198-204.

Tobin, J. (1969), 'A general equilibrium approach to monetary theory', *Journal of Money, Credit, and Banking*, vol. 1, no. 1, pp 15-29.

Turnovsky, S.J. (1990), 'The effects of taxes and dividend policy on capital accumulation and macroeconomic behaviour', *Journal of Economic Dynamics and Control*, vol. 14, pp 491-521.

US Department of Commerce,*National Income and Product Accounts(NIPA)*, 1959-88.

US Government,*Economic Report of the President*, Washington DC, 1978-90.

Whited, T. (1992), 'Debt, liquidity constraints and corporate investment: evidence from panel data', *Journal of Finance*, vol. 47, no. 4, pp. 1425-60.

Wildasin, D. (1984), 'The Q theory of investment with many capital goods', *The American Economic Review*, vol. 74, no. 1, pp. 203-10.